Anthony Trollope

Twayne's English Authors Series

Herbert Sussman, Editor

Northeastern University

TEAS 441

ANTHONY TROLLOPE
(1815–1882)
Photograph courtesy of the Department of Special Collections,
University Research Library, UCLA

Anthony Trollope

By Susan Peck MacDonald

University of California, San Diego

Twayne Publishers
A Division of G.K. Hall & Co. • Boston

Anthony Trollope

Susan Peck MacDonald

Copyright © 1987 by G.K. Hall & Co.
All Rights Reserved
Published by Twayne Publishers
A Division of G.K. Hall & Co.
70 Lincoln Street
Boston, Massachusetts 02111

Copyediting supervised by Lewis DeSimone
Book production by Janet Zietowski
Book design by Barbara Anderson

Typeset in 11 pt. Garamond
by P&M Typesetting, Inc., Waterbury, Connecticut

Printed on permanent/durable acid-free paper
and bound in the United States of America

Library of Congress Cataloging in Publication Data

MacDonald, Susan.
    Anthony Trollope.

    (Twayne's English authors series ; TEAS 441)
    Bibliography: p. 129
    Includes index.
    1. Trollope, Anthony, 1815–1882—Criticism and
interpretation.   I. Title.   II. Series.
PR5687.M27   1987   823'.8   86-25758
ISBN 0-8057-6945-5

Contents

About the Author

Susan Peck MacDonald received her Ph.D. from the University of Wisconsin, Madison, and has since taught at Eastern Connecticut State University, the University of Illinois, Champaign-Urbana, and the University of California, San Diego. Her publications include *Corrupt Relations: Dickens, Thackeray, Trollope, Collins and the Victorian Sexual System* (coauthored with Richard Barickman and Myra Stark), as well as articles on Jane Austen, Victorian science and literature, and composition. She is presently coordinating an interdisciplinary writing program at the University of California, San Diego.

Preface

Trollope's genius as a novelist has, ironically, resulted in his being generally ranked in the second tier of Victorian novelists—behind writers like Charles Dickens and George Eliot. By quantitative standards, he might have been ranked first among Victorians for his forty-seven novels, as well as his travel books, essays, and short stories. But though he was a more prolific novelist than either Dickens or Eliot (Dickens having written fifteen novels and Eliot seven), his productivity has made it more difficult for critics and readers to appreciate him fully. Beginning in his own day and continuing to some degree since, many critics seem to have felt that a man who could write so much must not be writing well. The image of the romantic genius driven to write by the pressure of his own imagination fits well with some writers, but Trollope, understanding it well, thumbed his nose at this romantic notion in his *Autobiography*. He emphasized instead the craft and industry needed for novel writing and in doing so managed to alienate some readers who missed the irony and exaggeration in his claims.

But even without the critical predisposition to distrust such untroubled artistic productivity, Trollope's enormous output would have created barriers to full appreciation of his work. He simply wrote too much for most of his contemporaries or successive readers to absorb fully and appreciate. In the case of a great novelist whose canon consists of relatively few novels (Jane Austen, for instance), readers are able to reread the entire canon and to participate in critical discussion about any part of it. But in Trollope's case, well-read critics may be familiar with only a fraction of the novels and therefore be unable to enter into critical dialogue with other critics who know a different portion of his work. No one can discuss all Trollope's writing with the same close attention that generations of readers have been able to devote to the complete works of Emily Brontë, Austen, or Dickens, and so there are many fine characters and incidents in Trollope's lesser novels that would have received far more attention had he been less prolific.

But it is not only the volume of Trollope's output that has kept him from being fully appreciated. The literary heritage of romanticism has resulted in two, often contradictory tendencies: an appreciation of the ordinary and the everyday that is associated with realism and, on the other hand, an appreciation of the bizarre, the exotic, the melodramatic, or the superhuman. Trollope is situated firmly in the realist camp (with exceptions to be discussed later) and so is likely to be unappreciated by readers who associate great writing with important or unusual events and characters. There is a tendency not to notice the subtlety or profundity of Trollope's realistic characters and events simply because they have a superficial ordinariness.

These difficulties in fully appreciating Trollope are related to the difficulties in writing about him. No study of this length could cover everything of importance in Trollope's work without resorting to bland generalities, but a study that covers only a few of Trollope's novels risks similar distortions. This study takes the middle course of attempting to discuss roughly half of Trollope's novels in order to give a sense of the range of his work while still discussing some of it in the detail its richness merits.

Another difficulty in writing about Trollope is that of balancing a thematic approach with a chronological one. Any simple chronological study of Trollope's immense output risks choking on its own immensity while any simple thematic approach must neglect either the variety of thematic concerns in the novels or the subtle changes in Trollope's concerns as he ages and responds to socioeconomic changes in his society. This study has attempted the middle course of discussing both thematic and chronological developments. Thus, while Trollope's narrator and realism remain fairly constant throughout his career, I have discussed them in greatest detail in terms of the early novels, despite their continuing importance. Similarly, though Trollope was sensitive to women's problems throughout his career, I have focused upon such problems only in the novels of the 1860s, perhaps the most interesting period for his studies of marriage and sexual relations. This approach may somewhat minimize the continuity of individual thematic concerns over his entire career or the continuity within the Barsetshire and Palliser series. But Trollope's thematic concerns shifted significantly enough over time that a combination of the chronological and thematic approach can give the truest picture of Trollope's development and his genius.

In this study I am indebted to many scholars and critics of Trollope's work who have striven to clarify small and large issues in the novels and to gain for Trollope the recognition he deserves. To Eastern Connecticut State University I am indebted also for a fellowship that allowed me to complete this study. In addition, I wish to thank my editor, Herbert Sussman, for his help and my husband, Kevin, and sons, Joshua and Geoffrey, for their support.

Susan Peck MacDonald

University of California, San Diego

Chronology

1864 *The Small House at Allington* and *Can You Forgive Her?*

1865 *Miss Mackenzie.*

1866 *The Belton Estate.*

1867 *The Claverings* and *The Last Chronicle of Barset.* Resigns from the Post Office.

1868 Travels on postal mission in the United States. Stands unsuccessfully for seat in Parliament.

1869 *Phineas Finn* and *He Knew He Was Right.*

1871 *Ralph the Heir.* Gives up Waltham House and visits son Frederick in Australia.

1872 Travels in Australia, New Zealand, and the United States, and settles in London on return.

1873 *The Eustace Diamonds.*

1874 *Phineas Redux.*

1875 Travels in Ceylon and Australia. *The Way We Live Now.* Begins *Autobiography.*

1876 *The Prime Minister.* Finishes *Autobiography.*

1877 Travels in South Africa.

1878 *Is He Popenjoy?*

1879 *John Caldigate.*

1880 *The Duke's Children.* Moves from London to Hampshire.

1881 *Dr. Wortle's School* and *Ayala's Angel.*

1882 Travels in Ireland. Dies in London, 6 December.

1883 *Mr. Scarborough's Family* and the *Autobiography* published posthumously.

Chapter One
Trollope's Life

In his *Autobiography* Trollope wrote that his childhood was "as unhappy as that of a young gentleman could well be, my misfortunes arising from a mixture of poverty and gentle standing on the part of my father."[1] The marriage of Fanny Milton to Thomas Anthony Trollope in 1809 began auspiciously enough; Thomas Trollope had achieved some distinction at Oxford and appeared to possess the abilities to make a successful career as a barrister. Between 1810 and 1818, Frances Trollope bore seven children, one of whom died at birth and four of whom died of consumption, leaving only the eldest son, Tom, and the fifth child, Anthony, to live past young adulthood.

By the time Anthony was born in 1815, Thomas Trollope's growing contentiousness was beginning to damage his career as a barrister, and since he still believed himself heir to a rich uncle, he continued to enter into ultimately ruinous expenses. He built an expensive house (Julians) in Harrow and had the family moved there when Anthony was still a baby.

When the rich uncle remarried and started a new family and when Thomas Trollope continued to estrange clients and other lawyers, the family moved to less expensive houses and Trollope ineptly attempted farming. Characteristically, he failed. Of his father's failures, Anthony later wrote:

He was a man, finely educated, of great parts, with immense capacity for work, physically strong very much beyond the average of men, addicted to no vices, carried off by no pleasures, affectionate by nature, most anxious for the welfare of his children, born to fair fortunes,—who, when he started in the world, may be said to have had everything at his feet. But everything went wrong with him. The touch of his hand seemed to create failure. He embarked in one hopeless enterprise after another, spending on each all the money he could at the time command. But the worst curse to him of all was a temper so irritable that even those whom he loved the best could not endure it. We were all estranged from him, and yet I believe that he would

have given his heart's blood for any of us. His life as I knew it was one long
tragedy. (p. 27)

Anthony's understanding of his father became useful later in his penetrating psychological studies of Mr. Crawley, Louis Trevelyan, and
others, but as a child he suffered greatly from the consequences of his
father's decisions.

Thomas Trollope's strongest ambition was to educate his sons well,
in the way he had been educated. With what Anthony charitably re-
ferred to later as "a certain aptitude to do things differently from
others" (p. 2), however, he sent his sons to Harrow as day students,
hoping thereby to gain an excellent education for his sons without an
expense that he could ill afford. Most of the other boys at Harrow
were boarding students from rich or aristocratic families, and the
seven-year-old Anthony, as he later tells us, found their contempt for
him a "daily purgatory" (p. 3), because he was beneath them socially,
wore worn-out clothes, and was dirty from his long walks to school.
Remarking that probably no other good writer has "had as wretched
a time and had to endure it for so long," C. P. Snow finds Trollope's
boyhood wretchedness more sustained than either Dickens's or Dos-
toyevski's.[2] The combination of social isolation, inferiority, and neglect from his family that Trollope experienced as a boy was later to
fuel his retreats into imagination, his aspiration to be socially accepted, and his desire to make money and gain respect. Perhaps without his boyhood misery he would never have become a novelist—at
least not the kind of novelist he became.

In 1827, after three years at Harrow and two at a private school in
Sunbury run by Arthur Drury, Anthony went to Winchester as part
of his father's ambition to qualify his sons to become fellows at New
College, Oxford, as he himself had been. Anthony suffered perhaps
less mortification at Winchester than at Harrow yet still felt himself
a pariah there. He was thrashed daily by his eldest brother, Tom, until the latter left.

Then, as Thomas Trollope's fortunes sank further, the resourceful
Frances Trollope conceived a scheme for restoring them. In 1827 she
(and several of the children) went to America with the idea of first
inspecting a utopian settlement in Tennessee and then opening a ba-
zaar in Cincinnati. Thomas Trollope and Tom joined them in Cincinnati for a while, leaving Anthony virtually alone in England. The
Cincinnati experiment failed utterly. The trip was ruinous to Henry's
health and to the family's finances, and in the meantime Anthony's

bills were not paid at Winchester. During one summer Anthony was even left alone at his father's law chambers, essentially abandoned by his family. He suffered especially from the other boys' knowing about his poverty; he later wrote of the Winchester period, "I had no friend to whom I could pour out my sorrows. I was big, and awkward, and ugly, and, I have no doubt, skulked about in a most unattractive manner. Of course I was ill-dressed and dirty. But, ah! how well I remember all the agonies of my young heart; how I considered whether I should always be alone; whether I could not find my way up to the top of that college tower and from thence put an end to everything?" (p. 8).

Then in 1830, after his father's return from America. Anthony was removed from Winchester—despite the possibility (unrecognized by Thomas Trollope) that he might have gained a fellowship at New College.[3] Instead he was returned to Harrow where he remained until the age of nineteen (1834). At first during that period he lived alone with his increasingly gloomy father and as a day student walked twelve miles daily along dusty lanes to Harrow—"dreadful" walks as he later described them (p. 13). Sir William Gregory later wrote of Trollope's schooldays at this time:

He was a big boy, older than the rest of the form, and without exception the most slovenly and dirty boy I ever met. He was not only slovenly in person and in dress, but his work was equally dirty. His exercises were a mass of blots and smudges. These peculiarities created a great prejudice against him, and the poor fellow was generally avoided. . . . I avoided him, for he was rude and uncouth, but I thought him an honest, brave fellow. He was no sneak. His faults were external; all the rest of him was right enough. But the faults were of that character for which schoolboys would never make allowances, and so poor Trollope was tabooed, and had not, so far as I am aware, a single friend. . . . He gave no sign of promise whatsoever, was always in the lowest part of the form, and was regarded by masters and by boys as an incorrigible dunce.[4]

When Frances Trollope returned to England in 1831, however, the family's fortunes improved slightly through the publication of her *Domestic Manners of the Americans* (1832). It was her first book, and she was then fifty. The improvement in fortunes was not lasting, though, and in 1834 the family moved to Bruges. Thomas Trollope, in increasingly poor health, was whisked away to Ostend (to prevent his arrest for debts) while the bailiff was actually in their house; after the Trollope belongings were repossessed, the family followed him to Bruges.

The household was reestablished in Bruges with three invalids. While Frances nursed her husband and two children who had consumption (Henry and Emily), she wrote the novels necessary to support them all. Henry and his father were particularly difficult invalids, but she persevered. Henry died later in 1834 and was followed early in 1835 by his father. Frances then returned to England where Emily died the following year. Yet in the midst of her troubles at Bruges, Frances had managed to have Anthony become a clerk at the General Post Office in London, a result of her friendship with Mrs. Clayton Freeling, daughter-in-law of the secretary to the post office (Sir Francis Freeling).

The Postal Service

At the age of nineteen, then, Trollope began seven years of service as a postal clerk, a period that lasted until 1841 when he was twenty-six.[5] During those years he began with an annual salary of ninety pounds, which gradually increased to one hundred forty pounds. He lived, for the most part, in somewhat ramshackle rooming houses and always exceeded his income. Later he explained that those years were neither creditable nor useful, that he was seen as a black sheep, and that he had a reputation for irregularity. In *The Three Clerks* (1858) he drew on such experiences to describe the haphazard process of a young clerk's admission to the postal service and a woman's coming to the office to ask when he meant to marry her daughter. Later in *Phineas Finn* (1869), he drew on his experience with a moneylender who visited him daily at the office to admonish him for his lack of punctuality. And in Johnny Eames's escapades at rooming houses and at the office in *The Small House at Allington* (1864) and *The Last Chronicle of Barset* (1867) he created the closest version of the feckless young man he then was—a "hobbledehoy" as he called both Johnny Eames and his younger self.

Though Trollope hated the life he led, his own idleness, and his job, still there is some reason to believe that his youth was not altogether wasted. Despite his reputation for unreliability and his willingness to antagonize superiors, Trollope tells us that he could write letters well (like his surrogate self, John Eames). And despite all he claims not to have known at the time, the list of his reading is fairly impressive; he knew the poets and historians, how his country was governed, and the names of bishops, heads of colleges, and cabinet ministers. He was familiar with Shakespeare, Byron, Scott, Milton, and Austen (his favorite novelist until Thackeray published *Henry Esmond*). Furthermore, he kept a journal for fifteen years from the time he was fifteen, and even earlier than that he had formed the habit of creating stories in his mind and then continuing them for weeks or even years—an excellent apprenticeship for the kind of novelist he was later to become.[6]

In 1841, after a serious illness and out of distaste for the life he was leading, Trollope applied for the position of postal surveyor's clerk in Ireland. He appears to have been given the position because no one else wanted it, because going to Ireland was looked upon as a demotion, and because his superiors at the Post Office in London were glad to be rid of him.

The position in Ireland paid him four hundred pounds a year, once travel allowances were figured in, so from the time he arrived in Ireland he was able to begin freeing himself from past debts and to avoid new debts. Perhaps more important, he enjoyed his work more, became more industrious than he had been in London, and acquired more self-esteem along with the respect of others. The *Autobiography* presents his move to Ireland as the "first good fortune" of his life (p. 49):

There had clung to me a feeling that I had been looked upon always as an evil, an encumbrance, a useless thing,—as a creature of whom those connected with him had to be ashamed. . . . I acknowledge the weakness of a great desire to be loved,—of a strong wish to be popular with my associates. No child, no boy, no lad, no young man, had ever been less so. And I had been so poor; and so little able to bear poverty. But from the day on which I set my foot in Ireland all these evils went away from me. Since that time who has had a happier life than mine? (p. 50)

Ireland allowed Trollope to demonstrate his efficiency and to mix work with physical activities. He rode his horse on much of his business and discovered a love of hunting. He balanced accounts, improved the efficiency of letter delivery, and investigated complaints. At the latter task, he was not universally popular because his manner was often aggressive and contentious, but at least he was not looked down upon as he felt he had been in England.

Within a year of the move to Ireland, he had met Rose Heseltine and become engaged to her. She was the daughter of a bank manager from Rotherham in Yorkshire. They did not marry until two years later (1844) because neither had any assets. Very little is said about her in the *Autobiography* or in accounts of Trollope's contemporaries, but she appears to have provided a stable domestic background and a good deal of editorial help as Trollope became a novelist. Biographers have had to speculate about her. Michael Sadleir assumes that we would know of it if Trollope's feelings for Rose had been more passionate: "Behind the blinds of Trollope's married life the fire of comfort, mutual self-esteem and genial affection glows unmistakably; but no flames leap."[7] C. P. Snow conjectures further: "Among the Trollope relatives a generation later, there were vestigial hints that she was not specially liked. . . . We are left with speculations. The present writer has to intrude his own: which is that she was very far from negligible, sharp-tongued, witty, a more coherent and in many ways tougher personality than her husband. Possibly too much so to give him a marriage ideal for his temperament." Snow theorizes that Trollope's "marvellous young women" (from Lucy Robarts and Mary Thorne to Mabel Grex) may have derived their "peculiar tantalizing appeal, at the same time subtle, funny and derisive" from Trollope's observation of his wife.[8]

Trollope began his Irish work in Banagher, but after his marriage the couple moved to Clonmel in Tipperary where in 1846 and 1847 two children, Henry Merivale and Frederick James Anthony, were born.

In 1843, after visiting a ruined Irish estate, Trollope began work on his first novel, *The Macdermots of Ballycloran.* The work progressed slowly before his marriage, then faster after it, so that he finished the novel in 1845 and saw it published in 1847. By the time he was transferred to England for a special two-year assignment in 1851, he had written two more works of fiction, the Irish novel *The Kellys and O'Kellys* (1848) and a historical novel, *La Vendée* (1850), as well as a play, *The Noble Jilt,* which he was advised in rather strong terms not to pursue. The Irish novels met with some kindness from reviewers but did not sell well, and in his *Autobiography* Trollope characterized all his early attempts as having no success and receiving no notice.

The Successful Novelist

No matter how one assesses his early work, however, it seems apparent that the move to England from 1851 to 1853 brought Trollope in touch with the rural England that inspired the Barchester series and led him in the direction of realizing his own particular genius. His job in England was to improve the efficiency of rural mail delivery, and he delighted in riding his horse (often as many as forty miles a day) over the countryside of western England. On a visit to Salisbury one day he conceived of *The Warden,* and though he was transferred back to Belfast before finishing it, he was at last headed in the direction of a successful literary career—at the age of forty.

In 1854 he was promoted to Postal Surveyor and transferred once again, from Belfast to Donnybrook (near Dublin) where he lived until 1859 when he finally was transferred back to England permanently. During those last years in Ireland, he was sent on missions to Egypt, Glasgow, and the West Indies, and visited his brother and mother in Florence, but in the meantime he continued with his Barchester novels.

The Warden was published by Longman early in 1855 and, without making much money, nevertheless seemed more successful than his earlier novels. So in 1855 he began *Barchester Towers* (1857). Then in 1857 he wrote *The Three Clerks,* in 1857 and 1858 *Doctor Thorne* (1858), and in 1858 *The Bertrams* (1859), despite the fact that he was in Italy and Egypt for much of 1857 and 1858.

The pattern of Trollope's success here becomes apparent. It was based upon depiction of rural England and its upper middle class or landed gentry, upon the speed with which he wrote, and upon his determination to make the most advantageous arrangements with publishers. After his modest success with *The Warden* and *Barchester Towers,* Trollope hoped to obtain more money from Longman's for *The Three Clerks.* When Longman balked at his terms, he tried another publisher (Hurst and Blackett). There he was kept waiting and so went to Bentley. Bentley published *The Three Clerks* but, when Trollope tried to sell *Doctor Thorne* there, Bentley appeared to be playing with him, so he took *Doctor Thorne* to Chapman and Hall.[9] Probably the fact that he had suffered so in his childhood from poverty and lack of status made him as an adult fiercely determined not to be mistreated by publishers and to earn as much money as possible from his work. The money appears to have been even more important to him as a form of recognition and respect than as a form of wealth.

In 1859 Trollope finally left Ireland and, for the first time in his life, became successfully integrated into a social community in England. How he managed before 1859 to create such wonderfully realistic British characters as Archdeacon Grantly remains something of a mystery, but in 1859 he bought a house at Waltham Cross near London and at last was able to spend time at the social clubs of London that literary men and publishers frequented. He continued with his full duties at the Post Office until 1867, hunted as often as twice a week, attended the London clubs, and yet found the time to write at least fourteen books between 1859 and 1867 when he resigned from the Post Office. Most of the books were about the Barchester milieu or the slightly more elevated, but still very British locale of the Palliser series.

Trollope continued to use Chapman and Hall; they published *Orley Farm* (1862), *Rachel Ray* (1863), *Can You Forgive Her?* (1865), *Miss Mackenzie* (1865), and *The Belton Estate* (1866) in this period. But he also experimented with serial publication and other publishers. His most important opportunity came in 1859 when he was asked late in October to contribute a novel to be serialized in the new magazine, the *Cornhill*, edited by Thackeray and published by George Smith. Thackeray himself had intended to supply the first novel but had procrastinated too long. If Trollope accepted their offer, he knew he would earn more money than ever before and be recognized as a novelist of first rank, but he would also have to produce the first installment by 12 December. In the meantime he was halfway through *Castle Richmond*, which had been sold to Chapman and Hall; in any case, Smith did not want *Castle Richmond* (an Irish story), preferring instead the English clerical milieu of Trollope's Barchester successes.

So despite his conviction that novels should be complete before being turned over to a publisher for serial publication, Trollope began work on *Framley Parsonage* without having finished *Castle Richmond* and then alternated work on them from November 1859 through the first half of 1860. *Framley Parsonage* was a success and led to the publication in the *Cornhill* of *The Small House at Allington* (1862–64) and *The Claverings* (1866–67).

In addition to several other magazine serializations, Trollope also experimented during this period by publishing several short novels not under his own name. He wrote *Nina Balatka* (1867) and *Linda Tressel* (1868) in an attempt to find out whether novels by established novelists continue to sell because of prestige or because of their intrinsic worth. When these two novels failed to sell well, Trollope concluded that the plight of a beginning novelist is difficult, though it seems equally likely that the short novel in a foreign setting was simply not suited to Trollope's genius.

Frustrations and Achievements of the Late Years

In 1867 Trollope resigned from the Post Office—perhaps because he was passed over for a promotion, though the reasons are not entirely clear. He still went on a Post Office mission to the United States in 1868 and then in 1868 stood for Parliament in Beverley.

The Beverley campaign was painful and frustrating and led to the campaigning scenes in *Ralph the Heir* (1871) in which Sir Thomas's unpleasant experiences with corruption in the Percycross election closely resembled Trollope's own. Neither Trollope nor his fictional character, Sir Thomas, was suited for the sorts of dishonesty and currying favor that a candidate needed to undertake. Sir Thomas's painful attempts to carry on an honest campaign demonstrated his unfitness for politics, a trait Trollope had discovered in himself. Perhaps as a result of his disappointment at Beverley and his conviction of the importance of Parliament, Trollope included more about politics in some of his subsequent novels—*Phineas Redux* (1874), *The Prime Minister* (1876), and *The Duke's Children* (1880)—but the optimistic view of politics that pervades *Phineas Finn*—a novel written before the Beverley election—disappears from his political novels after Beverley.

He also attempted editing a magazine. He had already been involved in establishing the *Fortnightly Review* earlier in the 1860s but undertook sole editorship of the new *St. Paul's Magazine* from 1867 until 1870. Sadleir sees the venture as an error in judgment that helped begin Trollope's decline with the public. He fell between two stools, Sadleir argues, in trying to combine literary scruples with commercial success, and when the owner of *St. Paul's* sold the magazine to another publisher, some of Trollope's copyrights then went to a firm with a lesser reputation, thereby damaging his reputation.[10]

The *St. Paul's* misadventure, along with other events, brought Trollope's rising earnings to a halt, and after 1870 his income began to decrease. Sadleir theorizes that the general public missed the cheerful tone of the Barchester novels and that intellectuals lost interest in Trollope when his publishers declined in reputation; after the mid-1870s neglect turned to indifference, the experimental late novels being received with dismay by devoted readers and neglect by a newer generation.[11]

In 1871 he gave up Waltham House partly because he and Rose were going to Australia to visit their son Frederick who was sheep farming there. At this time Trollope also seemed worried about supporting both an expensive house and hunting, when he no longer had his civil servant's pay and faced declining earnings from his novels. His sons had both added to his expenses. The elder son, Henry, first tried the law, then publishing, and finally became a man of letters, apparently well-liked but lacking his father's ambition. Frederick seems to have had more of his father's strong-mindedness but had also caused expense when his sheep farming failed to be profitable.[12] Trollope's relation with his sons appears to have been warmly affectionate, but their modest successes in life may have added to the worries of his last decade.

In 1872 Trollope returned to England and settled in Montague Square in London. He continued to write and to travel, making trips to Ceylon, Australia, South Africa, and Iceland in the late 1870s and then to Ireland in 1882 after the Phoenix Park murders renewed his interest in Irish problems. But his health was failing, and he was increasingly gloomy.

Despite the gloom, the decline in reputation, and the ill health of his last years, Trollope's achievements after the late 1860s were substantial. He wrote most of the Palliser novels after the decline began—*The Eustace Diamonds, Phineas Redux, The Prime Minister,* and *The Duke's Children.* He wrote a number of works of nonfiction—including *The Commentaries of Caesar* (1870), *Australia and New Zealand* (1873), *South Africa* (1878), *Thackeray* (1879), *The Life of Cicero* (1880), *Lord Palmerston* (1882), and *An Autobiography* (finished in 1876, published posthumously in 1883). In addition to this rather astonishing productivity, he wrote several non-Palliser novels that were rather neglected in his own day but whose strength would perhaps have sufficed to make another writer famous. Among them were *He Knew He Was Right* (1869), *The Way We Live Now* (1875), *Is He Popenjoy?* (1878), *Ayala's Angel* (1881), and *Mr. Scarborough's Family* (1883). But in Trollope's day the public could scarcely keep up with his output, and many readers were disturbed by the increased pessimism of the late novels. It has required the wisdom of retrospection and distance to discover ways in which the late models are equal and even in some respects superior to the early or middle novels.

The boy who suffered from social isolation, poverty, and even derision eventually became loved by friends and family, financially secure, and esteemed as a novelist; but the effects of Trollope's boyhood suffering never left him. He recognized this himself, as the *Autobiography* makes clear: "I have long been aware of a certain weakness in my own character, which I may call a craving for love. I have ever had a wish to be liked by those around me,—a wish that during the first half of my life was never gratified" (p. 133). He saw novel writing as a means for rising in status, in addition to its other pleasures: "But it is in the consideration which he enjoys that the successful author finds his richest reward. He is, if not of equal rank, yet of equal standing with the highest; and if he be open to the amenities of society, may choose his own circles. He without money can enter doors which are closed against almost all but him and the wealthy" (p. 175).

With the *Autobiography* and the perspective of distance to guide us, we can see how Trollope's early suffering might have led to insecurity and a manner that often appeared brusque, but many of Trollope's contemporaries had only his manner to guide their interpretations of him, and their accounts are contradictory. Trollope himself admits to loving feuds: "How I loved, when I was contradicted,—as I was very often and no doubt very properly,—to do instantly as I was bid, and then to prove that what I was doing was fatuous, dishonest, expensive, and impracticable! And then there were feuds,—such delicious feuds!" (pp. 236–37). Contemporary accounts may be found in which Trollope appears as a sort of wild man—talking louder than others, quarreling with superiors and equals, commanding his inferiors peremptorily. Yet other accounts give reason to believe that Trollope was sensitive, generous, and well liked by those who understood him. One of the most perceptive accounts by his contemporaries came from Julian Hawthorne:

[Trollope] seemed to be in a state of some excitement; he spoke volubly and almost boisterously. . . . He turned himself, as he spoke, with a burly briskness, from one side to another, addressing himself first to this auditor and then to that, his words bursting forth from beneath his white moustache with such an impetus of hearty breath that it seemed as if all opposing arguments must be blown quite away. Meanwhile he flourished in the air an ebony walking-stick, with much vigor of gesticulation, and narrowly missing, as it appeared, the pates of listeners. . . . His character was simple and straightforward to a fault, but he was abnormally conscientious, and keenly alive to others' opinion concerning him. It might be thought that he was overburdened with self-esteem, and unduly opinionated; but, in fact, he was but over-anxious to secure the goodwill and agreement of all with whom he came in contact. . . . He was incorrigibly strenuous to obliterate or harmonize the irreconcilable points between him and others; and since these points remained irreconcilable, he remained in a constant state of storm and stress on the subject.

It was impossible to help liking such a man at first sight; and I believe that no man in London society was more generally liked than Anthony Trollope. . . . He was a quick-tempered man, and the ardor and hurry of his temperament made him seem more so than he really was; but he was never more angry than he was forgiving and generous.[13]

Faced with the conflicting accounts of Trollope's personality, we may accept N. John Hall's conclusion that "Trollope, more than most men, prepared a face to meet the faces that he met. He assumed a role, put on a mask, acted out a part. It was a strategy to keep people, friendly or otherwise, at arm's length, to camouflage the insecurities and fears that lay so close to the surface. It was his way of coming to terms with his early years, which wretched circumstances together with his acute sensitivity to mental pain had made a horror."[14] The childhood sufferings that caused the adult Trollope to assume a mask, however, also caused him to work unceasingly—both at his Post Office job and at his novel writing. They must have been partly responsible for the sensitivity and complexity of the novels themselves. His readers may be tempted, then, to feel thankful, not that Trollope was forced to suffer, but that at least he came to terms with his sufferings by creating so rich a body of literature.

In 1880 Trollope and Rose left London and moved to Harting Grange near Petersfield. Late in 1882 they returned to London and on 6 December 1882 Trollope died, a month after having a stroke at a small dinner party in London.

Chapter Two

The Barchester Comedies: 1855–1860

The Barsetshire Setting

In the early Barsetshire novels, Trollope depicts a traditional society threatened by socioeconomic change.[1] Political reform endangers the security of the Barchester clergy in both *The Warden* and *Barchester Towers*. In the former, the threat arises from an apparent inequity in the income of the warden of Hiram's Hospital. Since the warden is a clergyman, the issue is taken up as part of the broader question of ecclesiastical incomes, but the inequity itself is the result of a rise in the value of land that has increased the warden's income. Victorian readers would have been familiar with such issues from contemporary debate about charitable trusts and church incomes.

In *Barchester Towers*, a new bishop (Bishop Proudie), his wife, and their chaplain (Mr. Slope) become threatening to the established clergy of Barchester because they side with the reformers on subjects like the wardenship. They are viewed with suspicion by the conservative Barchester clergy as outsiders, having more liberal political allegiances and more low-church religious views. The bishop is so tolerant as to stand for almost nothing (3), but his wife takes strong, low-church stands opposing sabbath travel and advocating sabbath schools.[2] She frowns upon other people's pleasures. She is also threatening because though she is a woman, she aspires to wield the powers of the bishop. Trollope indulges in some traditional, antifeminist satire in portraying Mrs. Proudie as a woman trying to exercise power, but she has other faults also. She and her sometime ally Slope are both seen as guilty of trying to usurp power while Mr. Harding's refusal to grasp at power is sanctioned.

Slope begins his stay in Barchester by preaching a sermon purposely designed to affront all the older, established clergy of Barchester. The mild-mannered Mr. Harding passes judgment on Slope by saying, "Christian ministers are never called on by God's word to in-

sult the convictions, or even the prejudices of their brethren; and . . .
religion is at any rate not less susceptible of urbane and courteous
conduct among men, than any other study which men may take up"
(8). Harding, other characters, and the narrator complain that Slope
is not a gentleman; the somewhat elusive quality of gentlemanliness
appears to symbolize for Trollope an ideal combination of character,
manner, and birth. While trying to browbeat Harding into refusing
the wardenship, Slope says, "It is not only in Barchester that a new
man is carrying out new measures and casting away the useless rub-
bish of past centuries. The same thing is going on throughout the
country. Work is now required from every man who receives wages;
and they who have to superintend the doing of work, and the paying
of wages, are bound to see that this rule is carried out. New men,
Mr. Harding, are now needed, and are now forthcoming in the
church, as well as in other professions" (12). The newcomers (the
Proudies and Slope) are judged in *Barchester Towers* to be at fault in
courtesy, in respect for tradition, and in tolerance or charity toward
others' views or actions, and the conservative forces of *Barchester Towers* emerge from the contest with a fairly easy victory, aided by the
obnoxiousnes of Mrs. Proudie and Slope.

In *Doctor Thorne*, however, the threat comes both from without and
from within the traditional segment of Barchester society. The Greshams, an old, landed, conservative family, have squandered most of
their wealth—and with it their power to influence others or act disin-
terestedly. At the opposite extreme, Sir Roger Scatcherd, a former
bricklayer who has risen to great wealth, can find no place for himself
either in the working class he has risen above or in the older class of
landed gentry, despite his land and wealth, so he has ruined his
health through alcoholism. But he has both the energy and the money
the Greshams lack and is able to lend them money. In this way Trollope suggests that the older, landed class needs to be revitalized by
the wealth and energy of new talents while the newcomers need the
stability and traditional values of the older class. This symbolic fusion
occurs when Mary Thorne, the illegitimate daughter of a Thorne and
a Scatcherd, inherits the Scatcherd wealth, marries Frank Gresham,
and restores the Greshams to fortune.

In *Framley Parsonage* the conflict is less simple, the threat to the
old order coming from within. Miss Dunstable, the newly rich heiress
of a quack-medicine fortune who first appeared in *Doctor Thorne*, reap-
pears again in *Framley Parsonage*, more securely absorbed into the

world of upper-class politics and social life and in danger of being corrupted by it. All the other major characters are from the older gen-teel classes, but they are now split into two camps. Lady Lufton is the major figure of one camp and represents traditional values like honesty, morality, and charity to one's neighbors. Of special interest in the other camp are the Duke of Omnium (a very rich Whig with questionable morals) and Mr. Sowerby (a debt-ridden member of Par-liament). Lady Lufton's son Lord Lufton and her young vicar, Mark Robarts, are both tempted by the life of casual elegance and sophisti-cation they associate with Sowerby. Consequently both are drawn into debt, Sowerby ruthlessly taking advantage of their naiveté to extract money from them. The consequences are particularly severe for Ro-barts because he compromises himself as a clergyman through a series of dealings with Sowerby and is eventually in danger of having all his belongings sold to pay the debts. Robarts is initially attracted to Sowerby because his casual style, his ability to ridicule, and his pleasure-filled life represent a very tempting alternative to the serious, ethical view of life Lady Lufton takes, but through the course of the novel, the shallowness and dishonesty of Sowerby's life are exposed and Mark returns to the Lufton fold.[3]

While the subject of change is crucial to his novels, understanding the complexity of Trollope's viewpoint involves going beyond simple statement of theme to an understanding of his novelistic techniques—his use of realism, narrative voice, and analogous plot structures—and of how thematic significance is created through those techniques.

Trollope's Realism

Perhaps the most important condition for comprehending and ap-preciating Trollope's novels is first understanding the nature of his "realism." *Realism,* a literary term common in the nineteenth century and in literary criticism since then, has such varied meanings, and the history of realistic fiction is so complex, that the term often cre-ates barriers to understanding.[4] Nevertheless, Trollope has always ap-peared to readers to be writing squarely in the tradition of realism. Nathaniel Hawthorne described Trollope's novels as being "just as real as if some giant had hewn a great lump out of the earth and put it under a glass case, with all its inhabitants going about their daily business, and not suspecting that they were being made a show of."[5] Trollope comments, in the *Autobiography,* that Hawthorne "describes with wonderful accuracy the purport that I have ever had in view of my writing. I have always desired to 'hew out some lump of the earth,' and to make men and women walk upon it just as they do walk here among us,—with not more of excellence, nor with exaggerated baseness,—so that my readers might recognise human beings like to themselves, and not feel themselves to be carried away among gods or demons" (123). Despite the complexity of varieties of realism, Trollope's novels are decidedly realistic in several senses of the term.

First of all, realism denotes a preference for depicting the middle ranges of sociey. Shakespeare, for instance, and most writers before the nineteenth century depicted extremes of high life (kings, nobles) or low life (clowns, rustics), the former being the subject of tragedy and the latter of comedy. By the nineteenth century, novelists had begun to focus more upon the middle ranges of society.[6] Yet even among Trollope's contemporaries, some novelists like Charles Dickens or Wilkie Collins were far more fascinated than Trollope with extremes of vice, deprivation, or virtue. Though Trollope has many characters from the upper levels of society, he has comparatively few from the lower end, and at the beginning of his career, at least, he was relatively unconcerned with extremes of conduct. Instead, the conflicts in his novels involve fairly ordinary dilemmas in courtship or interpersonal relationships among rather ordinary people of the upper classes.

Second, then, Trollope's realism avoids melodramatic events of the kind Dickens uses symbolically, preferring instead to focus on everyday dilemmas involving love, marriage, money, and social power. In the early novels particularly, the plot often is less important than the characters, a point the narrator frequently makes. The narrator often undercuts the importance of plot suspense by comments like the following: "But let the gentle-hearted reader be under no apprehension whatsoever. It is not destined that Eleanor shall marry Mr. Slope or Bertie Stanhope. And here, perhaps, it may be allowed to the novelist to explain his views on a very important point in the art of telling tales. He ventures to reprobate that system which goes so far to violate all proper confidence between the author and his readers, by maintaining nearly to the end of the third volume a mystery as to the fate of their favourite personage[11] (*Barchester Towers,* 15).

Although such statements by Trollope or his narrator are often made tongue-in-cheek, still readers have tended to appreciate Trollope more for his characters than for his plots.

Both these characteristics of Trollope's realism lead to a third aspect harder to define but one that accounts for much of Trollope's greatness as a novelist. In attempting to define the "shaping principle" of Trollope's art, Ruth apRoberts quotes a passage from one of Trollope's contemporaries, Bishop Connop Thirlwall: "The liveliest interest arises when by inevitable circumstances, characters, motives, and principles are brought into hostile collision, in which good and evil are so inextricably blended on each side, that we are compelled to give an equal share of our sympathy to each while we perceive that no earthly power can reconcile them. . . . What makes the contrast interesting is, that the right and truth lie on neither side exclusively: that there is no fraudulent purpose, no gross imbecility of intellect: but both have plausible claims and specious reasons to allege."[7] The ethical complexity Thirlwall here describes is, as apRoberts argues, central to Trollope's novels and particularly apparent in *The Warden.*

Realism in *The Warden* (1855)

The ethical dilemma and the plot of *The Warden* derive from the mixture of right and wrong in the attitude each of the characters takes toward the central question—whether the warden of Hiram's Hospital has a right to the large income he enjoys or whether the intention of the original donor, John Hiram, has been distorted by increases in land value since the original will was made in 1434. The old men who are sheltered by the hospital still have the same income they did under the terms of the will, but the warden, Mr. Harding, has a very comfortable income, much greater than that foreseen by John Hiram. John Bold is a reformer who feels that Hiram's intention has been distorted and that the warden's income represents corruption in the church. Bold takes this position on abstract grounds—despite his knowledge that the old men could not profit from a greater income and that Mr. Harding is a good man, not personally guilty of corruption.

The kind of abstraction Bold makes is characteristic also of the newspaper the *Jupiter* and two writers, Dr. Pessimist Anticant and Mr. Popular Sentiment, all treated with heavy-handed sarcasm by Trollope. Dr. Anticant (a caricature of Thomas Carlyle) is dismissed by Trollope's narrator as not recognizing "that in this world no good is unalloyed, and that there is but little evil that has not in it some seed of what is goodly" (15). Similarly, Mr. Popular Sentiment (a scarcely disguised caricature of Charles Dickens) rails in his novel

against an evil figure supposed to represent the warden, a man who
starves old men while enjoying luxury for his family. Trollope's narrator faults Mr. Sentiment because "the absurdly strong colouring of
the picture would disenable the work from doing either good or
harm" (15). Bold, the *Jupiter,* Dr. Anticant, and Mr. Sentiment all
in differing ways abstract the issue from the people involved and then
simplify it into a matter of good and evil, reform and tradition, or
justice and injustice. Trollope and his narrator, on the other hand,
refuse to ignore the complexities involved, and this refusal is at the
heart of Trollope's realism.

Unlike Dickens's characters, who are often either extremely good
or extremely evil, Trollope's characters who are on Mr. Harding's side
in *The Warden* are not necessarily right or good. Archdeacon Grantly,
Harding's son-in-law, is by no means disinterested in the position he
takes; he acts out of partisanship for the church, since the reformers
aim to reduce ecclesiastical incomes or make them more equitable,
and out of a desire to protect his father-in-law. The lawyer he pro-
cures for his side, Sir Abraham Haphazard, is equally partisan. Having been hired to defend Harding, Haphazard proceeds in adversarial
fashion to find a way for Harding to win the case. He takes his stand,
not on the right and wrongs of the issue, but on how the action is
worded.

Mr. Harding is caught in the middle between the abstract reformers, who appear to have right on their side but have ignored the personal element altogether, and his supporters, who seem not to care
about the right and wrong of the issue and yet support him without
understanding his personal needs. Harding would like to know which
is the right and which is the wrong course of action for him, but
right and wrong are not so easily abstracted from situations or from
people. In the end he resigns, and even his motives for doing so are
mixed; he resigns because no one can prove he is entitled to so comfortable an income, but also because he shrinks from public criticism.
His resignation serves a good end insofar as ecclesiastical abuse should
be scrutinized and avoided, but neither the old men nor anyone else
is really served by Harding's resignation. At the end of the novel, the
wardenship is empty, several of the old men have died without the
comforts of their spiritual advisor, and the vacancy has become a
source of contention both among the old men and, in the continuing
Barchester chronicle, among the clergy of Barchester.

Such mixed conditions are at the heart of Trollope's realism. He habitually portrays mixed motives within individuals—impulses and desires so hard for the individual to sort out that many of Trollope's characters spend a great deal of time introspectively picking through and revising their attitudes toward the conflicts in the novels.[8] He refuses to abstract issues from their context or rights and wrongs from the people whose lives are concerned, and he criticizes reformers like John Bold who do so. If Trollope takes sides at all in *The Warden,* he sides with Mr. Harding for his gentleness, his lack of contentiousness, and his decision to do what appears to him to be right. But the complexity of Trollope's realism is evident in that even his warmest supporters among literary critics cannot always agree upon whether Mr. Harding is right or why Trollope sympathizes with him.[9]

Trollope's Narrator

The complexity of Trollope's realism is increased by his use of narrative voice. Readers like Hawthorne who praised Trollope's "lump of earth" assume that Trollope's realism is simple and straightforward—an almost photographic copying of "real" life. But increasingly critics now realize that Trollope was not just hacking off a chunk of reality and presenting it as fiction. Henry James set the tone for much misunderstanding when he accused Trollope of being insensitive to art and of allowing his narrators to intrude inartistically, thereby drawing attention to the artifice of novel writing.[10] To appreciate, therefore, the complexity of Trollope's realism and to pass beyond the tangle of misunderstanding about his artistry, one must understand how Trollope uses his narrator.

The narrator has at least two functions—to reinforce ideas implicit in his story and to disrupt easy judgments.[11] At times the narrator reinforces the values apparent in the narrative in a fairly simple way, much as Dickens's narrators might. At the end of *The Warden,* for instance, the narrator reinforces a point made in the narrative, that the old men have gained nothing by the agitation for reform: "How gently did Mr. Harding try to extinguish the false hope of money which had been so wretchedly raised to disturb the quiet of the dying man!" (20). This simple reinforcement is the sort of "intrusion" that a younger generation of writers like James and Virginia Woolf considered illegitimate, inartistic, and old-fashioned. But such simple instances are, in any case, fairly rare.

More complicated interventions by the narrator serve to remind readers of perspectives they may overlook if too absorbed in the story. For instance, the narrator of *Doctor Thorne* often reminds us of the novel's central thematic issue, that love should not be distorted for the sake of money. Frank Gresham, the young romantic hero of the novel, is himself in need of money, and the plot involves his conflict between romance and the need to marry for money. In the end he marries for love and gains the money too, but Trollope is constantly careful to prevent our endorsing mercenary values. In one instance, after Frank's cousin (the third son of the noble De Courcy family) laments his lack of economic prospects, Frank suggests that his cousin must be happier as the younger son of an earl than as the eldest son of a plain squire. His cousin replies, "I wouldn't. . . . What chance have I? There's Porlock's as strong as a horse; and then George comes next. And the governor's good for these twenty years," to which the narrator immediately adds, "And the young man sighed as he reflected what small hope there was that all those who were nearest and dearest to him should die out of his way, and leave him to the sweet enjoyment of an earl's coronet and fortune" (4). The narrative comment here serves to block our sympathizing with the impoverished son, for the sake instead of reminding us that all gains of money are made at the expense of others. Later when Mary Thorne inherits the Scatcherd fortune (and therefore is able to marry Frank), this kind of reminder keeps us from glossing over the unhappiness of Sir Roger Scatcherd and his son's lives; if they had not both died of alcoholism, Mary would not have inherited.

Sometimes the length of the narrator's commentary serves to focus the reader's attention on an issue. Mr. Moffat is a minor character who seeks first to marry Augusta Gresham for her status and then abandons her in order to pursue the heiress Miss Dunstable. The narrator comments,

There is no doubt that the privilege of matrimony offers opportunities to money-loving young men which ought not to be lightly abused. Too many young men marry without giving any consideration to the matter whatever. It is not that they are indifferent to money, but that they recklessly miscalculate their own value, and omit to look around and see how much is done by those who are more careful. A man can be young but once, and, except in cases of a special interposition of Providence, can marry but once. The chance once thrown away may be said to be irrecoverable! How, in after-life, do men toil and turmoil through long years to attain some prospect of doubtful advancement! Half that trouble, half that care, a tithe of that circumspection would, in early youth, have probably secured to them the enduring comfort of a wife's wealth. (18)

The narrator's sarcasm here encourages us both to disapprove of young men's seeking to marry for money and to understand how society operates. That understanding leads to sympathy at the same time that we are encouraged to disapprove. Again Trollope has complicated our responses in the way he criticizes Dr. Pessimist and Mr. Popular Sentiment in *The Warden* for failing to do.

An even more blatant intervention occurs when the narrator steps outside the time frame of the novel to tell us of something that happens four years after the novel ends. Within *Doctor Thorne,* the aristocratic Lady Amelia De Courcy counsels her weaker cousin, Augusta Gresham, against marrying Mortimer Gazebee, a young man of lower social standing than the Greshams or De Courcys. After showing us Augusta's weakness in abandoning Gazebee on her cousin's advice, the narrator informs us that Lady Amelia herself later marries Gazebee. The effect is to make us pity Augusta, to undercut the De Courcy pretensions, and to invite our sympathy for young women who are socially and economically pressed to marry. The narrator's relevation thus serves to broaden our understanding of an issue in the novel. This habit of the Trollopian narrator can be summarized in the words of Geoffrey Harvey: "He made the garrulous, intrusive voice of the author the basis of his realism. In his manifold references to work, social and cultural institutions, leisure pursuits, moral attitudes and the like Trollope's narrative voice builds into the novel those laws by which its world operates, laws similar to those in the real world, in order to convince the reader of its truth without his having to refer outside the novel itself."[12] Thus Trollope's narrative voice provides an extension of the themes of his story, helping to create and extend their implicit meaning.

But at the same time, the narrator also seems to have another function, a distancing or disrupting function. This is perhaps most apparent in his undercutting of novelistic conventions. Repeatedly, the narrator draws attention to the artifices of the novel in a way that disrupts the reader's engagement in the story, complicates interpretation, and draws attention to the artificiality of the very conventions through which he is simultaneously operating. In *Doctor Thorne,* for instance, after a rather slow introduction, the narrator comments, "I quite feel that an apology is due for beginning a novel with two long dull chapters full of description. I am perfectly aware of the danger of such a course. In so doing I sin against the golden rule which requires us all to put our best foot foremost" (2). Of Frank Gresham, he writes, "He would have been the hero of our tale had not that place been pre-occupied by the village doctor. As it is, those who please may so regard him. It is he who is to be our favorite young man, to do the love scenes, to have his trials and his difficulties, and to win through them or not, as the case may be. I am too old now to be a hard-hearted author, and so it is probable that he may not die of a broken heart" (1). In both instances, he undercuts the novel's pretention to being about "real" people by drawing attention to the artifice involved in writing introductions or constructing romantic plots, but doing so simultaneously gives the reader the sense of a reality that goes beyond fictional convention. Similarly at the end, when he lists all the marriages and tells the fate of all his characters, he undercuts the conventions he adheres to in saying, "And of whom else must we say a word? Patience, also, of course, got a husband—or will do so. Dear Patience! it would be a thousand pities that so good a wife should be lost to the world" (47). That comment "or will do so" undercuts the comic convention of happy marriage by mocking it at the same time it creates the illusion that Patience Oriel exists outside his novel.

The narrator also distances the reader, at times, from false pretensions the characters may have. Frank Gresham is urged by his mother and aunt to court the wealthy Miss Dunstable, but because he is in love with Mary Thorne, Frank refuses—usually—to do more than converse in a friendly way with Miss Dunstable. At one point, however, he becomes carried away by learning of other men's courtship of Miss Dunstable and starts to act as aggrieved as if he were genuinely courting her. The narrator comments, "And then he sighed again, so that it was piteous to hear him. He was certainly an arrant puppy, and an egregious ass into the bargain; but then it must be remembered in his favour that he was only twenty-one and that much had been done to spoil him. Miss Dunstable did remember this, and therefore abstained from laughing at him" (20). It is characteristic of Trollope's narrator here and elsewhere that he can simultaneously reveal a character's weaknesses and still create sympathy for him.

In Trollope's early novels, the narrator most often uses gentle forms of commentary on a character's weakness to broaden and correct while still maintaining sympathy, but even in the early novels there are occasions when one hardly knows where the narrator stands. In *Framley Parsonage,* ecclesiastical incomes once again become an issue. The Framley parson, Mark Robarts, seeks to enlarge his income (already 900 pounds a year) while a neighboring clergyman, Mr. Crawley, scarcely survives on 130 pounds. The narrator's commentary moves quickly from one position to another:

One cannot conceive that . . . any approximation could have been made, even in those old mediaeval days, towards a fair proportioning of the pay to the work. At any rate, it is clear enough that there is no such approximation now. And what a screech would there not be among the clergy. . . . Ecclesiastical work to be bought and paid for according to its quantity and quality!

But, nevertheless, one may prophesy that we Englishmen must come to this, disagreeable as the idea undoubtedly is. . . .

How pleasant it was, too, that one bishop should be getting fifteen thousand a year, and another with an equal cure of parsons only four! . . . There was something in it pleasant, and picturesque; it was an arrangement endowed with feudal charms, and the change which they have made was distasteful to many of us. A bishop with a regular salary, and no appanage of land and land-bailiffs, is only half a bishop. Let any man prove to me the contrary ever so thoroughly—let me prove it to my own self ever so often— my heart in this matter is not thereby a whit altered. One liked to know that there was a dean or two who got his three thousand a year (14).

This voice, apparently meandering from reason to sarcasm to nostalgia, then introduces us to the poverty that endangers not only the health but also the sanity of Mr. Crawley and his family. The narrative voice has served to increase the number of possible viewpoints on the issue and to balance each; thus the narrator creates a dialectic, or "opens" the novel as James Kincaid would put it, rather than closing off meaning by coming down on the side of reform or tradition.[13]

This kind of dialectical opening up of the novel, as well as the other kinds of narrative interventions serve to deemphasize plot and keep us from reading unreflectively. The interventions serve to increase the complexity of the thematic and ethical issues in the novels, to increase sympathy, and to provoke thought. In the end they reinforce the novels' realism, despite their apparent artifice, by increasing complexity at the expense of convention and suggesting that life is too large to be understood simplistically.

Plot Structures in *Barchester Towers* (1857), *Doctor Thorne* (1858), and *Framley Parsonage* (1861)

Although Trollope's plots may seen subordinate to his characters, his plot structures are nevertheless extremely important in creating the thematic complexity of his texts. There are, to begin with, in Trollope two characteristic kinds of plots—a romance plot and an initiation plot. The romance plot resembles others of its kind throughout Western literature; it has a happy ending with one or more marriages. Since the romance plot usually centers upon a young woman, Trollope's novels contain many interesting studies of young women, and since his romance plots are usually dialectically related to one or more other plots, the heroine's development usually has some significance for the second plot.

The initiation plot varies in its content somewhat more than the romance plot. The conventional nineteenth-century initiation story is that of a young man's passing from adolescence to manhood through finding his place in society. Trollope uses a young man's initiation for his plot quite often, but he also creates similar stories for older men. In *The Warden* Mr. Harding must reexamine his position in life and the ethical issue forced upon him by socioeconomic change. In *Barchester Towers* the newcomers (Slope and the Proudies) force the established clerical men (Grantly and his faction) to reaffirm their own values and strengthen their power. Once again, the plot involves how the clergy of Barchester will deal with changes that threaten the socioeconomic status quo. In *Doctor Thorne* there is a double plot for the male characters—the initiation plot of young Frank Gresham and the story of Doctor Thorne's attempt to secure a place for Mary Thorne without acting unethically. In *Framley Parsonage* there is an initiation story about Mark Robarts—his temptation to succumb to the value and way of life of the faction represented by Sowerby and the Duke of Omnium, the trials he undergoes, and his return to the values represented by Lady Lufton. While the male plot is less conventional than the romance plot in that it may involve older or younger men, ethical dilemmas or initiation into society, Trollope's novels usually contain at least two dialectically interrelated plots, one about a man's struggle in the world and the other about a young woman's.

This interrelationship between the two plots comes from the fact that male and female characters share common ends as well as common dilemmas. For instance, in *Barchester Towers* the war between clerical factions is mirrored by the war for Eleanor Bold's hand in marriage, and Arabin, the champion of the conservative Grantlyites, wins Eleanor just as he wins the deanship.

In *Doctor Thorne*, marriage, economic security, and initiation are similarly related. Mary Thorne, though she is illegitimate, inherits money from her uncle, Sir Roger Scatcherd, the representative of new money. The theme of conflict between an older, established upper class (represented by the Greshams and De Courcys) and new, moneyed people is tied to the romance plot. In the novel's major and minor plots, the possibility of marriage between two people of different classes raises questions about the place of love in marriage, the ethics of marrying for money, and the balance between change and tradition. Frank Gresham comes of age after his father has incurred so many debts that Frank needs to marry money. He wants to marry Mary for love, however.

The events of the novel in essence test the three major characters, Frank, Mary, and Doctor Thorne. Frank must remain true to his love, must mature, and must refuse to marry for money. Mary must remain true to her love, must not debase herself by currying favor with those of Frank's family who are opposed to her, must accept with pride her ambiguous social status, and must at the same time prove herself worthy of acceptance into the class the Greshams belong to. The doctor must continue to act as social, medical, and economic advisor to both the Scatcherds and Greshams without doing anything to advance Mary's interests, even though he alone knows that Mary can be Sir Roger's heir and he alone is in a position to influence both sides covertly. In the end, since all three major characters have met the tests the plot held for them, the novel is happily resolved, with Frank and Mary marrying, Mary inheriting the Scatcherd money, and the money serving to clear the Gresham debts. Thus the male and female plots are interrelated.

Coherent interrelationship of plots is particularly important in novels with multiple plots, so two devices that Trollope uses to connect plots are analogous scenes and analogous plots.[14] *Barchester Towers* contains a number of analogous scenes, for instance. Since the clerical plots revolves around whether the reform-minded newcomers to Barchester—Bishop Proudie, Mrs. Proudie, and the chaplain Mr. Slope—will oust the old guard (Archdeacon Grantly and Mr. Harding, especially), Trollope creates a series of scenes in which one faction ousts the other from a room. The first of these skirmishes comes when Grantly and Mr. Harding pay their first visit to the Proudies. The house that Grantly has grown up in—that his father (the former bishop and Mr. Harding's dearest friend) has lived and died in—has been transformed by the interlopers. Quite naturally Grantly and Harding recoil at the new decorations as well as at the hostility of the newcomers themselves. When Mrs. Proudie and Slope complain about repairs needed for the house, Grantly and Harding are astonished and do little more than escape in order to gather their forces.

Shortly thereafter, the Proudies hold an evening reception, but in this scene it is the Proudies who are bested and must flee. Madeline Neroni, a delightfully improper Victorian who functions in the novel to unmask pretence, takes possession of the Proudie sofa, becomes the center of attention, and then looks on with amusement when her brother Bertie, while moving the sofa, accidentally rips Mrs. Proudie's dress, forcing her to flee the room.

A third skirmish occurs in the bishop's room when the bishop and Slope make a brief and doomed attempt to conquer Mrs. Proudie. They succeed only temporarily because later, in the bedroom, Mrs. Proudie regains her customary ascendance over her husband.

Later in the novel, the Thornes of Ullathorne hold a fete in which a social climber named Mrs. Lookaloft penetrates into the drawing room rather than go to the places outside reserved for the lower classes. Then Madeline Neroni, once again taking possession of a parlor sofa, drives the formidable, aristocratic Lady De Courcy from the room. Throughout the novel, Madeline Neroni receives the men of Barchester in her own parlor and at times drives them from her by embarrassing them, most noticeably in the case of Slope.

The skirmishes in rooms invite comparison and help link together seemingly disparate characters and events; more important, they are linked to the novel's questions about houses and positions. Archdeacon Grantly had grown up in the bishop's house and hoped to be reinstated there as bishop. Mr. Harding hopes to be reinstated as warden of Hiram's Hospital. Mr. Arabin, "tired of his Oxford rooms and his college life" (20), is lured to the modest parsonage of St. Ewold's but later acquires the deanship. Thus throughout *Barchester Towers* the struggle men and women undergo to find a "place" in life is literally carried on in places—rooms and houses—with the rewards being "place" in both senses of the word: those who are successful gain positions and houses.

Plots and characters are also used analogously to create meaning, to define issues, and to create the kinds of complexity characteristic of Trollope's realism. In the early novels, there is often a central character whose dilemmas are reflected in minor characters. In *Doctor Thorne,* for instance, Mary Thorne's plight in loving a young man who lacks the money to marry her is shared in different ways by two minor characters, Augusta Gresham and Miss Dunstable. Augusta's unfortunate engagement to Mr. Moffatt demonstrates the folly of trying to marry for money while her willingness to let her cousin coax her out of marrying Mortimer Gazebee demonstrates the folly of weakness in love as well as the folly of attaching too much importance to aristocratic status. At the opposite extreme, the sensible heiress, Miss Dunstable, turns away a number of young men interested merely in her money, though she would willingly marry a man who loved her and whom she loved. The unhappy events of Augusta and Miss Dunstable's stories help to define the dilemmas of the main plot while also counterbalancing its happy ending; not all romances, Trollope suggests, end happily.

The same form of balance between major and minor plots or between parallel characters is characteristic of Trollope's other early novels. In *Barchester Towers* Arabin and Slope counterbalance each other, as aspirants both for Eleanor's hand and for the deanship.[15] Eleanor's three suitors each help to define attitudes toward power, money, religion, and courtship.

In *Framley Parsonage* the romantic plot centers upon Lucy Robarts and Lord Lufton. His mother, Lady Lufton, wants him to marry Griselda Grantly, the beautiful and statuesque daughter of Archdeacon Grantly. Griselda is repeatedly silent at times when Lucy might be witty, and since Lufton has the same kind of wit, it is understandable that Lufton and Lucy are well suited. Griselda, by contrast, would rather dance than talk and eventually marries Lord Dumbello, whose silence or dumbness is indicated by his name. The contrast between Griselda and Lucy helps to define not only which one Lufton should marry, but also which one his mother should prefer. For much of the novel, she clings to her preference for Griselda but eventually realizes that Lucy is a more appropriate daughter-in-law for her.

Similarly, in *Framley Parsonage* Mark Robarts's trials are defined— and undermined—by the trials of Mr. Crawley. At the same time that Trollope's characteristically compassionate realism encourages us to understand the temptations besetting Robarts, he also shows us in Crawley a man who retains the integrity of a clergyman despite far greater trials. But Trollope's parallelism, as usual, works in both directions. Robarts's pleasant and accommodating personality—the same personality that has led him into Sowerby's snares—helps to demonstrate the difficulties of Mr. Crawley's stiff-necked pride. Together, the two clergymen suggest the wisdom of the middle ground—a personality neither too pliant nor too stiff, an integrity that is sound but not painful to others.

In the early novels, then, Trollope's realism, his narrative voice, and his use of parallel characters or plots all tend toward the same end; they avoid simplicity and encourage readers to see the complexity of human ethical and social dilemmas. They often suggest a middle ground, a balance between extremes.

Chapter Three

Variations on the Novel of Romance

The marriages that constitute the endings of *Barchester Towers, Doctor Thorne,* and *Framley Parsonage* show how important to Trollope's early novels was the traditional romantic plot structure, which begins with courtship, follows struggles through obstacles, and ends in happy marriage. The progression from Eleanor Bold to Mary Thorne to Lucy Robarts is a movement toward a more complex heroine, but the central romance plot in each case revolves around misunderstandings or economic and social problems. The heroine herself knows her own mind (Eleanor somewhat less than others), and her marriage at the end is presented as happy and fairly unproblematic. The social problems that might impinge on the romance are relegated either to the background or to minor plots; within the major plot the problems that existed at the beginning are resolved.

After *Framley Parsonage* (1861), however, we find greater complexity entering into Trollope's use of the romance plot. His heroines and heroes begin to have greater psychological depth, his endings contain more ambivalence, and the socioeconomic environment impinges more forcefully upon the characters. *Rachel Ray* (1863), *The Small House at Allington* (1864), *Can You Forgive Her?* (1864), *Miss Mackenzie* (1865), and *The Belton Estate* (1866), while not equally complex or problematic, demonstrate three similar clusters of interrelated motifs: (1) repression, often in relation to religion; (2) the "cross-grained" heroine and the status of women; and (3) the two-suitors theme.

Rachel Ray (1863)

Rachel Ray deserves consideration alongside more important novels like *The Small House at Allington* and *Can You Forgive Her?*, not because of the heroine herself, but because of the treatment of the community's attitude toward women and courtship. Rachel's widowed sister, Mrs. Prime, is a sour, repressive Evangelical who associates cheerfulness and beauty with sin (1). Her mother, Mrs. Ray, is a weak, easily led woman who, despite her own cheerful nature, has acquiesced in Mrs. Prime's moral views. When Luke Rowan begins courting Rachel, both Mrs. Ray and Mrs. Prime are aghast—and manage to communicate their fears to Rachel. Of Mrs. Ray, Trollope writes,

When she heard of a wedding . . . she rejoiced greatly, thinking that the son of Adam had done well to get himself married. But whenever it was whispered into her ear that any young man was looking after a young woman,—that he was taking the only step by which he could hope to find a wife for himself,—she was instantly shocked at the wickedness of the world, and prayed inwardly that the girl at least might be saved like a brand from the burning. A young man, in her estimation, was a wicked wild beast, seeking after young women to devour them, as a cat seeks after mice. (1)

This view comes in part from Mrs. Ray's clergyman, Mr. Comfort—so named because, unlike Mrs. Prime, he is not very strict about applying his religious teaching to daily life. Among them, however, with Mrs. Ray's natural fears and naive faith in Mr. Comfort's teaching, Mr. Comfort's more worldy fears about Luke's reliability, and Mrs. Prime's life-denying evangelicalism, they raise obstacles to Rachel's engagement (until Luke proves his fidelity and his economic safety at the end).

Mrs. Prime is at first presented as an object for animosity, but as the story progresses her own parallel courtship and engagement reveal new dimensions and turn her into a more complex character. By contrast, in *Barchester Towers* Mrs. Proudie's similar low-church views are objects for both animosity and laughter. Mrs. Prime initially is treated more seriously than Mrs. Proudie, Mrs. Prime's views being potentially more dangerous to the heroine and hero. Mrs. Proudie remains stable, always trying to repress others, never dangerous enough to succeed, and never (at least until *The Last Chronicle of Barset*) taken seriously as a character who has either needs or psychological complexity of her own.

Mrs. Prime, however, is less simple. She is transformed in *Rachel Ray* in a way that shows Trollope's sensitivity to the complexity of Victorian women's lives. She becomes engaged to a clergyman, Mr. Prong, whose religious views resemble hers—only to find that her engagement threatens her freedom. Though we do not sympathize with Mrs. Prime when her love of power leads her to spy upon and chastise

Rachel, we begin to sympathize with her when she realizes that Mr. Prong will marry her only if he has control over her money. By the time she decides, at length, to retain her freedom and her money, she is no longer an object of satire.

In these ways *Rachel Ray,* though it is seemingly a simple romantic comedy, raises questions about the status of women and about the ways in which their socioeconomic status can produce fear, repressiveness, or even perversity in them.

The Small House at Allington (1864)

The seeming perversity of Lily Dale, her determination to act in a way that all her friends think will cause her unhappiness, is the central subject of *The Small House at Allington,* a novel that uses the elements of the romantic novel in order to reexamine them. Instead of focusing upon courtship, the novel foreshortens the courtship of Lily Dale and Adolphus Crosbie, announces their engagement in chapter 5, and from there proceeds to Crosbie's doubts about the engagement, his jilting Lily, his subsequent misfortunes and remorse, and Lily's sorrow and obstinate refusal to relinquish her commitment to Crosbie.

Lily is one of the most complex female characters in Trollope's early novels; she demonstrates one facet of his genius as a psychological and sociological novelist—his understanding of the ways in which individual temperament and social circumstance can mingle to shape personality.[1] Lily's loyalty to Crosbie may be seen as, on the one hand, a reflection of her proud and persevering nature. She has the pride and obstinacy characteristic of the Dale family (her uncle, Christopher Dale, also having never married after an early disappointment). But more than temperament is involved. The idealization of romantic love and the concept of purity and faithfulness it entailed for Victorian women create the potential for misfortune when combined with the temperament and circumstances of a Lily Dale.

Lily's style of loving, to begin with, is not what we think of as characteristically Victorian; she is not prudish, secretive, cautious, or bashful about her love. Trollope frequently depicts—and appears to approve of—young women (Mary Thorne, Lucy Robarts, Glencora Palliser, Violet Effingham) who seem delightfully liberated from the gloomy evangelical constraints that weighed so heavily on Rachel Ray. But Lily's openness becomes part of her undoing. She shows "bold assurance" in her love and "seemed to declare to all the world that she was about to be married immediately" (9). Interpreting the traditional female bashfulness during engagement as a sign of distrust, Lily deliberately acts proudly and openly, but doing so creates unease in Crosbie and later makes Lily vulnerable:

Poor Lily! . . . Had she known his wish she would have wrapped up her love carefully in a napkin, so that no one should have seen it,—no one but he, when he might choose to have the treasure uncovered for his sight. And it was all for his sake that she had been thus open in her ways. She had seen girls who were half ashamed of their love; but she would never be ashamed of hers or of him. She had given herself to him; and now all the world might know it, if all the world cared for such knowledge. Why should she be ashamed of that which, to her thinking, was so great an honour to her? She had heard of girls who would not speak of their love, arguing to themselves cannily that there may be many a slip between the cup and the lip. There could be no need of any such caution with her. (9)

After taking a stand that in itself may have been admirable, however, Lily finds it a matter of pride to retreat (13).

In other circumstances, such loyalty and openness might have served her quite well. In *Doctor Thorne,* for instance, Mary is rewarded for her loyalty to Frank Gresham, her faithfulness epitomizing the ideal behavior of a young woman in love. But when Lily applies the same loyalty in different circumstances after being jilted, we are able to see how the ideals of romantic love encouraged something like self-destructiveness in Lily, turning her natural pride and perseverance into something more like obstinacy or perversity. Trollope thus partially subverts the ideology of romantic faithfulness with Lily.

After Crosbie jilts her, it becomes a matter of pride for Lily not to admit that she was wrong in loving him. But not only pride is involved; the Victorian love ideal also works against Lily's happiness in holding it to be shameful for a woman to love more than once, in associating purity with constancy. As Lily says late in the novel after John Eames asks her to marry him, "I still love [Crosbie] better than all the world. . . . I should be disgraced in my own eyes if I admitted the love of another man, after—after—. It is to me almost as though I had married him. I am not blaming him, remember. These things are different with a man" (54). And to her mother she says, "In my heart I am married to that other man [Crosbie]. I gave myself to him, and loved him, and rejoiced in his love. When he kissed me

I kissed him again, and I longed for his kisses. I seemed to live only that he might caress me. . . . I cannot be the girl I was before he came here. . . . I am as you are, mamma,—widowed." (57).

Lily, thus, is too proud to admit that she was wrong and too influenced by Victorian ideals of maidenly modesty to be able to love a second time. But another element is also involved; Lily is a strong-willed young woman in a society that does not provide many legitimate outlets for female power (hence the unpleasantness of Mrs. Proudie's or Mrs. Prime's uses of power). Through her perverse refusal to do what all her friends think will make her happy, Lily manages to convert a defeat into a victory of sorts. The passages above occur in a chapter entitled "Lilian Dale Vanquishes Her Mother" (57), and indeed Lily vanquishes all her family in that she manages to have her way. At first they give way to her out of pity: "at the present period of their lives all Lily's requests were sacred" (54). Then as she assumes the status of widow, she also throws off the need for subservience proper to an unmarried young woman. So she arrives at a position of power in which she can say only partly facetiously to her mother, "I shall have my own way; shall I not? That is all I want; to be a tyrant over you, and make you do my bidding in everything, as a well-behaved mother should do" (57).

Trollope further elaborates upon and complicates his theme through the interplay of his parallel plots and parallel characters in *The Small House at Allington*.[2] One minor female character's story undermines the romantic ideology that Lily has accepted. Amelia Roper is a young woman of the struggling lower middle class, a class with some pretensions to respectability but with precarious economic circumstances that often rendered respectability beyond its reach. Amelia, who is over thirty, is not so young as Lily, so sheltered (she has had to work as a milliner in Manchester), or so well provided for. Lily's uncle eventually settles money on Lily out of pity and so that she can remain unmarried without dropping out of the class she belongs to. Amelia, however, must marry for economic security. Some of the Victorian love ideal, thus, is seen to apply only to Lily's more fortunate circumstances; Amelia cannot afford to remain faithful to a jilting lover, to be coy and let a man make all the advances, or to refuse to marry a suitor who could provide for her (as Lily refuses to marry Johnny). Lily's actions appear to be an unaffordable luxury from Amelia's point of view.

Thus in the beginning of the novel, Amelia pursues John Eames in a way that almost makes her a stock figure of comedy, but as the novel progresses we are led to ask why Johnny should seem heroic in loving Lily but half pursuing Amelia while Crosbie seems villainous in jilting Lily for Alexandrina. Similarly, we are led to feel uncomfortable about sympathizing with Lily and laughing at Amelia. By the end—as is characteristic of Trollope's realism—Amelia has achieved a dignity that covertly undermines Lily's position. Amelia has fallen genuinely in love with Johnny, has been refused by him, and has found it all the more difficult but still necessary to pursue marriage for security. She says to Johnny, "I wish I'd never seen you. . . . I didn't think ever to have cared for a man as I have cared for you. It's all trash and nonsense and foolery. . . . It's all very well for young ladies as can sit in drawing-rooms all their lives, but when a woman has her way to make in the world it's all foolery" (59). Characteristic of Trollope's realism is this ambiguity; he first tempts us to judge Amelia conventionally—to laugh at her or look down upon her—and then complicates that reaction, teaching us to find it impossible to take a simple view toward her.

Adolphus Crosbie's story is similar to Amelia's in that we are tempted, in mid-novel, to scorn Crosbie for jilting Lily—to wish upon him all the unhappiness that Lily's friends wish upon him—but when his unhappiness is realized, we find ourselves unable to separate sympathy and disapproval. Trollope seems to have had a fascination for vacillating characters. He shows Crosbie right after his betrothal coming to doubt the wisdom of marrying a young woman with no dowry, then drifting into an engagement to Alexandrina De Courcy—partially through weakness and partially through ambition. After he jilts Lily and is on the verge of marriage, Crosby comes to realize that he would have preferred Lily, and with poetic justice he discovers that his income is even more precarious with the De Courcy connection. He gains nothing by his marriage and loses a great deal.

Some of Trollope's contemporaries might have handled Crosbie's story differently. George Eliot had a way of meting out rather strong justice to men like Tom Tulliver, Casaubon, or Grandcourt, despite all her sympathy for them (they drown, die of a heart attack, and drown, respectively). Dickens (like Mr. Popular Sentiment of *The Warden*) tended to divide characters into good and bad. But Trollope tends to refuse us the comfort of either dividing characters into good and bad or punishing them in ways that console the reader. *The Small House at Allington* is an uncomfortable novel; in the romantic tradition, it nevertheless refuses marriage to its heroine, triumph to its hero (if Johnny Eames is its hero), and the satisfactions of defeat for its villain, or of having a villain to defeat. Instead Trollope shows us Crosbie, a fairly ordinary man torn between ambition for money and social status on the one hand (ambitions precluded by a marriage to Lily) and the Victorian ideal of domesticity and love on the other. His disappointments among the De Courcys are shown, not in the melodramatic mode (with great suffering or a sense of tragic self-betrayal), but in the realistic mode with small discomforts, petty demands, and a sense of emptiness combining to sour his existence. Both Crosbie and Lily have been betrayed by the ambitions customary to their sexes.

Can You Forgive Her? (1864)

The complexity with which Trollope handles the romance in *The Small House at Allington* is present again in *Can You Forgive Her?*, but on a larger scale. Unlike the earlier *Doctor Thorne* with its one central romance and conventional ending, *Can You Forgive Her?* has three romance plots, at least two of which are central.[3] The change in plot structure from *Doctor Thorne* (or *Barchester Towers*) to *Can You Forgive Her?*, then, consists of an increase in the number of perspectives from which the central issues are examined. *Can You Forgive Her?* is, moreover, the first of the six-volume Palliser series, and so the complexity or even ambiguity of single novels in the series increases through Trollope's continued examination of his characters over time in the series as a whole.

The title itself refers to Alice Vavasor who is "cross-grained"—Trollope's adjective for young women who act seemingly against their best interests and ignore the advice of friends. She resembles Lily Dale (though she is not so charming) and demonstrates a perversity like Lily's, although she jilts her suitors, rather than remaining stubbornly constant to one as Lily does. Her perversity seems obvious from a synopsis of the plot: she has been engaged to her cousin George Vavasor, but has broken the engagement; she becomes engaged to John Grey and breaks that engagement; then she becomes engaged once again to George, and finally marries John Grey. As in the case of Lily, however, this seeming perversity is viewed as more than a simple character flaw once it is related to the status of women.

Trollope's awareness of the issues surrounding the status of women

was characteristically both perceptive and ambivalent. In lectures and
occasionally in his narrative voice he demonstrates little sympathy
with the women's rights movement then beginning to surface. He often ridicules characters like the Miss Pallisers, learned but unmarried
ladies. But at the same time, his women characters' dilemmas reveal
his profound, if not entirely conscious or explicit, understanding of
the problems producing the women's rights movement.[4] In the following passage, his narrator appears intolerant of Alice's hesitations;
having argued that poor marriages may sometimes results from lei-
surely engagements as well as from rapid ones, he says,

That Alice Vavasor had thought too much about it, I feel quite sure. She
had gone on thinking of it till she had filled herself with a cloud of doubts
which even the sunshine of love was unable to drive from her heavens. . . .
She had gone on thinking of the matter till her mind had become filled with
some undefined ideas of the importance to her of her own life. What should
a woman do with her life? There had arisen round her a flock of learned ladies
asking that question, to whom it seems that the proper answer has never yet
occurred. Fall in love, marry the man, have two children, and live happy
ever afterwards. I maintain that answer has as much wisdom in it as any
other that can be given;—or perhaps more. (11)

On the basis of such passages, as well as Alice's occasional prudery
and lack of charm, a number of readers and critics have disliked or
misunderstood the Alice Vavasor plot.[5] But Alice's story is again
characteristic of the narrative techniques we have seen in *The Warden,*
for instance, or the treatment of characters as diverse as Mrs. Prime
and Adolphus Crosbie. Trollope begins with a problem that we
might make a conventional judgment about: in this case, the problem
is Alice's wild vacillations about marriage. A conventional judgment
might be that Alice is crazy (or else that, naively, Trollope did not
know what he was about) and that we cannot forgive or sympathize
with her. That judgment is reinforced by the narrator's occasional
conservatism about women and marriage, as well as Trollope's statements elsewhere on the women's issue. But, as we have seen, his narrator often functions to complicate, not to simplify, and while the
narrator appears to urge marriage upon Alice, elsewhere the novel amply justifies Alice's hesitations.[6]
    To begin with, Alice desires some kind of independence, but in
her day there were few or no fulfilling roles open to women of her
class outside of marriage. The Miss Pallisers clearly do not lead lives
so fulfilling that Alice might want to imitate them; their cousin Jef-

frey says of them, "Being women they lead a depressed life, devoting themselves to literature, fine arts, social economy, and the abstract sciences. They write wonderful letters" (23). They do not, however, even read the replies to their letters, a sign of the emptiness of their activity. Another possible model for Alice is her cousin Kate, but Kate is as much at a loss about her life as Alice, finding no meaning for herself other than in sacrifice for her brother.

One other kind of independence within Alice's reach is the negative kind gained from opposing her father or her more distant female relatives. Perversity of this sort is about as much freedom as Alice can assert for herself.

So in her longing for something better, Alice attempts to achieve excitement and fulfillment vicariously by sharing the activities of a man's life. She becomes reengaged to her cousin George Vavasor, not because she loves him, but because he is running for Parliament and may therefore lead an exciting life, a life she can help create by giving him her money.

Alice's objections to John Grey center upon the issues of independence and fulfillment. Her romantic or sexual attraction is all for John Grey and not for George, but she objects to John because he is patronizing and because his life seems too dull. There are a number of instances in which Grey seems patronizing. The gentlemanliness of his silence on the subject of her traveling with Kate and George disturbs Alice; she sees him as so sure of himself that he need not stoop to arguing the issue with her. He is equally certain about his own life: "he always spoke and acted as though there could be no question that his manner of life was to be adopted, without a word or thought of doubting, by his wife" (3).

When Alice begins to withdraw from their engagement, he treats her as if she were sick or childlike. Alice interprets this as condescension: "There was something in the imperturbed security of his manner which almost made her angry with him. It seems as though he assumed so great a superiority that he felt himself able to treat any resolve of hers as the petulance of a child" (11). His superiority and self-command imply an inequality between them that Alice feels will threaten her independence, and a second issue is also involved, the issue of whether his life-style will suit her:

He had never asked her to argue with him. He had not condescended so far as that. Had he done so, she thought that she would have brought herself to think as he thought. . . . But she could not become unambitious, tranquil,

fond of retirement, and philosophic, without an argument on the matter,—
without being allowed even the poor grace of owning herself to be convinced. If a man takes a dog with him from the country up to town, the
dog must live a town life without knowing the reason why. . . . But a
woman should not be treated like a dog. (63)

There is, thus, ample evidence in the text that Alice is right to be
wary of John Grey—that he is condescending, does not allow her
equality in decision making, and ordinarily leads a rather placid, private life that might not suit her. But Alice's jilting of Grey forces
him to change somewhat; he becomes less condescending, more capable of being shaken in his own self-certainty, and he finally decides
to run for Parliament, thereby balancing his private life with a more
public one, a balance the novel endorses.[7]
    Despite these salutary changes in Grey, however, Alice's feelings
and actions are further complicated by vulnerabilities inherent in the
Victorian female role. Alice desires independence, but she hates to be
unfeminine, so while jilting her suitors, she nevertheless struggles
with the guilty feeling that she has acted impurely in doing so. Thus
in the midst of her attempts at independence, she still places very
little value on herself; she asks herself, "What after all did it matter?"
(34), and is weak enough to give up her money to George even after
she realizes his worthlessness.
    It is largely through Alice's feelings of guilt and unworthiness that
George is able to prey upon her; at one point he demands money of
her in a letter so insolent that a healthy reaction would have been to
repudiate his claims. Instead, the narrator tells us, "The unparalleled
impudence of this letter had the effect which the writer had intended.
It made Alice think immediately of her own remissness,—if she had
been remiss,—rather than of the enormity of his claim upon her"
(60).
    While Alice gets into her troubles partially through a lack of self-
esteem, once she has jilted both her suitors, she feels even more undeserving and guilty. She says repeatedly that she has "no right to happiness after the evil that she had done" (70) and that she cannot
forgive herself. The major reason for her guilt must, again, be seen
in relation to the roles prescribed for Victorian women of her class.
Her feelings are described as follows:

She knew that she had done wrong. She knew that she had sinned with that
sin which specially disgraces a woman. She had said that she would become

the wife of a man to whom she could not cleave with a wife's love; and, mad with a vile ambition, she had given up the man for whose modest love her heart was longing. She had thrown off from her that wondrous aroma of precious delicacy, which is the greatest treasure of womanhood. She had sinned against her sex; and, in an agony of despair, as she crouched down upon the floor with her head against her chair, she told herself that there was no pardon for her. (37)

Somewhat like Lily Dale, Alice suffers from the Victorian notion that a pure woman can love only once, with great devotion, and not marry a man whom she cannot love. Both Alice's guilt about the "delicacy" of her actions and her judgment that she has been "vile" in ambition, thus, are related to the roles prescribed for women in her day.

Nevertheless, as is typical of Trollope's characters, Alice's personality is rich in complexity; while she appears to consider herself undeserving, she still resists the pity or forgiveness of others because she does not want to be inferior to them. Since pity and forgiveness involve condescension and Alice has always battled against condescension, she suffers more from the pity and forgiveness of others than she might from their scorn or her own guilt. She delays betrothing herself to Grey a second time, possibly for that reason—because by refusing to be forgiven she can avoid condescension. Indeed, Alice is one of Trollope's most complex women characters and reveals the depth of his understanding of the way a Victorian woman's life could be shaped by the desire for control over her life within the context of a social ideology that denies her such control. With Alice (as with Lily earlier and with Emily Wharton later in *The Prime Minister*), we see strong-minded women acting in ways that appear neurotic because of the clash between what they want for themselves and the social ideology that constrains them.

The second heroine of *Can You Forgive Her?*, Glencora Palliser, if perhaps no more complex than Alice, has certainly appealed more to readers. Glencora's wit, vivacity, and courage make her, as Robert Polhemus writes, "one of the greatest of . . . nineteenth-century women in English fiction."[8] In many respects, Glencora's story provides parallels to Alice's. Both (along with the widowed Mrs. Greenow) have to choose between two suitors, one of whom appears dull and the other romantic. Alice is tempted by the seemingly romantic George Vavasor, just as Glencora is tempted by the seemingly romantic Burgo Fitzgerald. George and Burgo are also parallel, and the apparent romantic excitement they offer is in both cases finally rejected with George and Burgo's wildness coming to be understood as selfishness, recklessness, and self-destruction.

Alice and Glencora also both struggle with problems of self-esteem, Glencora experiencing moments of "madness" in which she seems "resolute to throw herself from a precipice" (42) by running off with Burgo. She "did not count herself for much" and even says to her husband, "What matters it whether I drown myself, or throw myself away by going with such a one as him [Burgo], so that you might marry again, and have a child? . . . I'd die willingly" (58). The guilt she feels at not producing the heir Palliser wants (together, perhaps, with an emptiness she herself feels at not having a child) leads her to moods of self-destructivness similar to those Alice feels because of her supposed sins.

The issue of purity that Alice violates is an issue also for Glencora in that she loves a man she is not married to, contemplates running off with him, and is in the meantime going through the motions of a marriage without love (the kind of marriage both Lily Dale and Alice felt to be prohibited by the ideal of female purity). Yet Glencora's apparent sins are partially the fault of the guardians who forced her to marry Palliser. Thus the issue of female purity has many dimensions, as Glencora points out: "And, as for female purity! Ah! What was their idea of purity when they forced me, like ogres, to marry a man for whom they knew I never cared? . . . How;—when [Burgo] kissed me, and I could hardly restrain myself from giving him back his kiss tenfold, could I respect myself? But it is all sin. I sin towards my husband, feigning that I love him; and I sin in loving that other man, who should have been my husband" (67).

Glencora's dilemma differs from Alice's, however, in that Glencora is not sexually attracted to Palliser as Alice is to John Grey and that Glencora desires love even more strongly than independence, unlike Alice who must choose between love and independence: "To love and fondle someone,—to be loved and fondled, were absolutely necessary to [Glencora's] happiness" (24). But Palliser, while he is good, just, and important as a political figure (of the sort Alice could appreciate), is cold, without knowing that he is cold, and humorless, given to explaining politics to Glencora at one in the morning when he comes to bed after long hours of study (43).

Glencora's dilemma is resolved, however, after the crisis created when she almost runs off with Burgo and then explains her temptation to Palliser. He realizes for the first time some of what she needs and then sacrifices his most cherished ambition to take her to Europe and away from temptation. In doing so he conquers her by tenderness (59), and on their trip she finally becomes pregnant, the symbol of their developing marital love.

Both before and after their new harmony Glencora provides an example of a woman who uses wit to negotiate some degree of freedom in restrictive circumstances. Alice uses rebellion and perversity for similar reasons, to escape the confines of a marriage she fears, but Alice's rather straitlaced temperament does not charm the reader in the way that Glencora's wit does. Even after the enormous sacrifice Palliser makes for her, Glencora can be found poking fun at her husband and occasionally driving him to exasperation in exchanges like the following:

[Mr. Palliser said,] "I think we had better make up our mind to stay a month at Baden."
"But why should we make up our minds at all?" his wife pleaded.
"I like to have a plan," said Mr. Palliser.
"And so do I," said his wife,—"if only for the sake of not keeping it."
"There's nothing I hate so much as not carrying out my intentions," said Mr. Palliser. (68)

The narrator next explains that Palliser bears up well under ridicule but that he can afford to do so: "it must be acknowledged that he behaved very well. But, then, he had his own way in everything. Lady Glencora did not behave very well,—contradicting her husband, and not considering, as, perhaps, she ought to have done, the sacrifice he was making on her behalf. But, then, she had her own way in nothing" (68). Her wit, in other words, is partially a survival device, a mechanism for creating some freedom and excitement out of otherwise rather constrained circumstances.

Perhaps because her wit gives her the freedom she needs, perhaps because Palliser's developing affection and her baby give her the love she requires, Glencora's marriage in the end is presented to us, not as a perfect, idealized union, but as a marriage with growing strength, one that Trollope was to trace with great interest through the rest of the Palliser series. Of Glencora's adjustment to her marriage by the end of *Can You Forgive Her?* Trollope wrote in the *Autobiography*, "The romance of her life is gone, but there remains a rich reality of which she is fully able to taste the flavour" (p. 154). It was characterictic of Trollope to be fascinated by characters' ability to adapt to their circumstances and by the richness of reality left beyond romance. No characters, perhaps for that reason, were more important to him than the Pallisers; as he wrote, "By no amount of description or asseveration could I succeed in making any reader understand how much these characters with their belongings have been to me in my latter life . . ." (*Autobiography*, p. 151).

Miss Mackenzie (1865)

Miss Mackenzie resembles Trollope's other novels of this era not only in its thematic concerns, but also in its transformation or probing of the conventions of the romantic novel. He wrote in his *Autobiography*: "*Miss Mackenzie* was written with a desire to prove that a novel may be produced without any love; but even in this attempt it breaks down before the conclusion. . . . I took for my heroine a very unattractive old maid, who was overwhelmed with money troubles; but even she was in love before the end of the book" (pp. 157–58). Yet while his engagement with the romance tradition was strong enough, apparently, to force his heroine's story into a romance mold, Trollope persisted in reexamining and, at times, undercutting the romance tradition in the process.

Once again forces of repression are present. There are an overbearing mother (Lady Ball) and a repressive religious woman (Mrs. Stumfold), but the theme of repression is perhaps most interesting in its connection to issues surrounding the status of women. Miss Mackenzie comes into her money at the age of thirty-six after years of having no existence other than as nurse to her brother. Her inheritance upon his death causes her to be approached by four suitors, none of whom would have done so had she not had money. Her reactions toward them are colored by her lifelong insecurity and self-depreciation—a devaluation encouraged by a society in which men are more likely to inherit money than women, women may sacrifice themselves to nurse their male relatives, and women are sometimes taught to think the desire for pleasure or independence is sinful. From all these sources of insecurity Margaret Mackenzie struggles to extricate herself and even arrives at an acceptance of her own sexuality in a scene Robert Polhemus describes as "showing a particular combination of insight and delicacy possibly beyond the range of any other Victorian novelist."[9]

In this scene she is looking in the mirror, admitting she is old:

> but as her fingers ran almost involuntarily across her locks, her touch told her that they were soft and silken; and she looked into her own eyes, and saw that they were bright; and her hand touched the outline of her cheek, and she knew that something of the fresh bloom of youth was still there; and her lips parted, and there were her white teeth; and there came a smile and a dimple, and a slight purpose of laughter in her eye, and then a tear. She pulled her scarf tighter across her bosom, feeling her own form, and then she leaned forward and kissed herself in the glass. (9)

Since Margaret holds very low expectations of what she is entitled to from life and yet also desires romance, she is at first tempted to accept one of her inferior suitors. One suitor, Mr. Rubb, comes from a lower class (he is in "trade"), but at least he holds out to her a greater chance of happiness than the repressive Stumfoldians. The result is some rather interesting speculation on Margaret's part about the importance of class—or the rather dubious benefits of being a lady. Her friend Miss Baker is a lady but is so repressed by her own notions of ladylike behavior and by the evangelical Stumfoldians that Margaret is tempted to think happiness might be found by abandoning class status. Margaret asks herself, "After all, what what the good of being a lady? . . . She recognized perfectly the delicacy and worth of the article. . . . But, then, might it not also be very well not to be a lady; and might not the advantages of the one position be compensated with equal advantages in the other? . . . There was something about Miss Baker that was very nice; but even Miss Baker was very melancholy, and Miss Mackenzie could see that that melancholy had come from wasted niceness. Had she not been so much the lady, she might have been more the woman" (9). In the end the novelist allows Miss Mackenzie a suitor of her own class—John Ball—so that she need not decide between being a lady and being a woman.

Few (if any) novelists have chosen for their romantic hero a figure like John Ball—an aging man with a large family (nine children, the oldest at Oxford), and perpetually worried about money until he learns that the heroine has unjustly (though innocently) inherited money that legally was his. We should not take too seriously Trollope's suggestion that he tried and failed to produce a novel without love; his particular genius lay in his ability to take conventional elements then transform them and probe their complexities as he does in *Miss Mackenzie*.

The Belton Estate (1866)

A repressive religious woman (Mrs. Winterfield) and a repressive mother (Lady Aylmer) make their appearances again in *The Belton Estate,* both trying to determine who the heroine will or will not marry. Once again the heroine, Clara Amedroz, resists these women's attempts to control her and, rather like Alive Vavasor, fluctuates between suitors as part of her attempt to carve out some independence for herself.

Initially Clara becomes engaged to Captain Aylmer, but before long she realizes she loves Will Belton more. Yet like Lily Dale and Alice Vavasor, Clara is too proud to admit her error—and too ashamed to admit that a woman's feelings can be transferred from one man to another. It seems almost indelicate to her to agree to marry Will so shortly after having agreed to marry another.

As in *The Small House at Allington* and *Can You Forgive Her?,* Clara's uncertainty and seeming perversity are related to the status of women. Her brother has squandered the family fortune and then committed suicide, and since the estate is entailed upon a male heir, Clara cannot inherit it. Her aunt Mrs. Winterfield fails to provide for Clara because her male heir, Captain Aylmer, seems more important. So Clara is likely to be penniless unless she marries. She has a claim on both Aylmer and Will's money, but she resents her dependence upon receiving money from one or the other. She would like to be economically independent and to feel that in choosing to marry she chooses freely, not out of economic necessity. Similarly, she does not want to marry Aylmer just because Mrs. Winterfield wished it, nor does she want to accept orders from an overbearing prospective mother-in-law.

Trollope's portrait of Clara Amedroz probably adds nothing to the complexity already present in Lily Dale or Alice Vavasor, but his use of the two-suitors theme in *The Belton Estate* is worth noting in light of the shortcomings of the romantic heroes (Crosbie, George Vavasor, and Burgo Fitzgerald) and the virtues of the more cautious suitors (Eames, Palliser, John Grey, and John Ball) in the preceding novels. Captain Aylmer is the cautious suitor—slow to anger, neither very generous nor passionate. He vacillates about marrying Clara and once engaged does not rush to set a wedding date. He stays away when Clara's father dies, not perceiving Clara's need for comfort. And he is easily led by his domineering, moralistic mother.

Will Belton is Aylmer's opposite—quick to fall in love but constant in his passion. He is generous in defeat but easily angered. He steals a kiss (even when Clara is still engaged to Aylmer) because he cannot help himself, while Aylmer scarcely shows any physical interest in Clara. Will rushes to her side when her father dies and would give over the estate to her even if she were to marry Aylmer. He can hardly refrain from proposing to her either the first or the second time and, once engaged, wants the shortest possible engagement. As genial, uncomplicated, and passionate a hero as Victorian literature has to offer, Will Belton is one of Trollope's answers to the repressive Evangelicals who feared dangerous young men and their passions.

It is central to the nature of Trollope's realism and his novelistic genius to create our sympathy for a hero like Will Belton in one novel and for a figure like Mr. Palliser in another, just as he is able to make us understand and sympathize with women even when they are acting self-destructively. Probably his finest novel of this period is *Can You Forgive Her?*; Trollope himself wrote that the Palliser novels were among the best work of his life and that any lasting success he might have would "probably rest on the character of Plantagenet Palliser, Lady Glencora, and the Rev. Mr. Crawley" (*Autobiography*, 155 and 300). But there is a wealth of observation and insight even in his less well known romantic novels of this period.

Chapter Four
Love and Money

Despite the growing complexity of the courtship plots of Trollope's novels in the early sixties, their heroines either triumph or at least hold the center of the stage. During the same period, however, Trollope began to write novels with a darker view—with more somber endings, with women less innocent, and with a growing pessimism about the relation between love and money.

Orley Farm (1862)

Orley Farm, though it was written before more comic novels like *Rachel Ray, Can You Forgive Her?, Miss Mackenzie,* and *The Belton Estate,* develops themes that dominate the more pessimistic novels of the late sixties and seventies. Its heroine Lady Mason is a widow in her forties, whose problems are far more difficult to resolve than those of the earlier heroines. She is not a young heroine like Mary Thorne who triumphs over economic and social barriers or like Clara Amedroz who overcomes self-imposed psychological barriers to achieve a happy marriage. Lady Mason's story illustrates four themes that become increasingly important to Trollope by the late sixties and the seventies: (1) the importance of a woman's innocence and the retribution that awaits her if she sins, (2) the destructive effects of money upon love, (3) the difficulty of telling truth from deception, and (4) the force of parental love.

Orley Farm begins twenty years after Lady Mason has forged a codicil to her husband's will in order to secure Orley Farm for her son. Evidence is brought to light that makes it possible to retry her for perjury (or forgery) so that Lady Mason is forced to undergo great suffering and, above all, to fear the consequences for her son. The novel very clearly illustrates the idea that crime does not pay, that retribution awaits sinners. In the end, the son for whom she has committed the crime not only feels disgraced and forced to relinquish the property, but also is alienated from her to some extent; and her own life

has been sacrificed by perpetual fear of detection. The narrator makes
it clear that the sin has carried with it its own punishment:

> She longed for rest,—to be able to lay aside the terrible fatigue of being ever
> on the watch. From the burden of that necessity she had never been free since
> her crime had been first committed. . . . In every word she spoke, in every
> trifling action of her life, it was necessary that she should ask herself how
> that word and action might tell upon her chances of escape. She had striven
> to be true and honest,—true and honest with the exception of that one deed.
> But that one deed had communicated its poison to her whole life. Truth and
> honesty—fair, unblemished truth and open-handed, fearless honesty,—had
> been impossible to her. Before she could be true and honest it would be nec-
> essary that she should go back and cleanse herself from the poison of that
> deed. (2:23)

In several novels of this period, Trollope's narrator sums up by saying
one cannot touch pitch without being defiled.

Though Trollope has a variety of male figures who are warned not
to touch pitch, nevertheless the moral character of his women is
treated somewhat more stringently than that of his men. His ambivalence about the roles of women takes the form of sometimes showing
the injustice of woman's lot or the damaging consequences of conventional views of women but at other times of adopting the conventional Victorian view that women are—or should be—more moral
than men, i.e., chaste, faithful without wavering, truthful, not mercenary, and innocent.[1] This idealized view of women contains its own
ambivalence, amply illustrated, for instance, in John Ruskin's conviction, stated in 1865, that women were meant to be purer than men,
partly in order to uplift men.[2] The concern with woman's faithfulness, honesty, and innocence appears even more strikingly in later
novels, such as *The Claverings* (1867) and *The Eustace Diamonds*
(1873), but it is present here in Sir Peregrine Orme and his daughter-
in-law's reactions to Lady Mason's guilt. Sir Peregrine, a neighbor of
Lady Mason's who is in his seventies, has come to love her and wants
to protect her, never dreaming that she is other than innocent. When
he proposes to marry her, she at first agrees but later realizes that she
must not subject him to the disgrace that might result if her guilt
became known. So she confesses her guilt to him to explain why they
should not marry. Sir Peregrine is shattered by her confession—partly
from a fear that his daughter-in-law, Mrs. Orme, will be tainted by
association with Lady Mason:

He had ventured to love;—to increase the small number of those . . . whom
he regarded as best and purest,—and he had been terribly deceived. He had
for many years almost worshipped the one lady [Mrs. Orme] who had sat at
his table, and now in his old age he had asked her to share her place of honour with another. What that other was need not now be told. And the world
knew that this woman was to have been his wife! . . . He had ventured his
all upon her innocence and her purity . . . and he had lost.
    . . . Her [Lady Mason] he could forgive for deceiving him. He had told
his daughter-in-law that he would forgive her [Lady Mason]; and it was a
thing done. But he could not forgive himself in that he had been deceived.
He could not forgive himself for having mingled with the sweet current of
his Edith's life the foul waters of that criminal tragedy. . . . The woman
[Lady Mason] had been very vile, desperately false, wicked beyond belief,
with premeditated villany, for years and years;—and this was the woman
whom he had wished to make the bosom companion of his latter days! (2:19)

Slowly through the novel, Sir Peregrine widens his sympathies and
comes to love Lady Mason despite her sin. It is clear in this and in
later Trollope novels that the woman who once sullies her innocence
by a sin can never regain the esteem she has lost. But at the same
time it is characteristic of Trollope to make Lady Mason more human
and more sympathetic through her sorrow, just as Sir Peregrine also
becomes more human and sympathetic through his pity for her.
    The sin most common in Trollope's portraits of women at this pe-
riod is that of marrying for money or marrying without love. Lady
Mason describes her past as follows to Mrs. Orme:

You can never understand what was my childhood, and how my young years
were passed. . . . Till he [her son Lucius] lay in my arms I had loved nothing. From my earliest years I had been taught to love money, wealth, and
property; but as to myself the teachings had never come home to me. When
they bade me marry the old man because he was rich, I obeyed them,—not
caring for his riches, but knowing that it behoved me to relieve them of the
burden of my support. . . . But then came my baby, and the world was all
altered for me. What could I do for the only thing that I had ever called my
own? Money and riches they had told me were everything. (2:20)

Though Trollope appears sympathetic to the plight of a woman like
Lady Mason, he repeatedly shows that women who marry for money
without coming to love their husbands are unable to erase their errors
once they recognize that they might have chosen a better course. He
reinforces his theme in *Orley Farm* by comic minor characters

(Moulder, Dockwrath, and Kantwise, in particular) whose commercialism parallels the commercialism of marrying for money.[3]

The importance of woman's honesty and innocence is paralleled by the importance of being able to tell lies from truth. The legal world of *Orley Farm* displays a number of ironies. The system is set up to discover the truth and to protect the innocent, ostensibly, but it also functions to protect the guilty. The witnesses in Lady Mason's trial for perjury are truthful and innocent but are made to look guilty by the badgering barrister, Mr. Chaffanbrass, while Lady Mason's innocence of demeanor has deceived people about her guilt for twenty years. The jury finds her innocent in spite of the guilt that seems obvious to the judge, to all the lawyers employed on both sides, and to most of Lady Mason's friends. The theme of the power of falsehood to deceive becomes even more apparent in *The Eustace Diamonds* and *The Way We Live Now;* in *Orley Farm,* Lady Mason is so sympathetic a character that it is easy to be misled, but in Trollope's later novels far less admirable characters display an even greater ability to deceive others.

Finally, *Orley Farm* resembles some of Trollope's later novels in its depiction of the strength of parental love. Lady Mason has not only committed a crime but lived a life of self-sacrificing reticence in order to protect her guilty secret, and when she is faced with the second trial (the trial central to the novel itself) she exerts almost superhuman strength to attempt to survive her difficulties with the least damage to her son. The strength of her love and the irony that her sacrifice instills so little gratitude in her son are themes that come to be quite important as Trollope ages.

The Claverings (1867)

The Claverings is structured around questions of marriage and money and, implicitly, the issue of female innocence. The central contrast is between Julia Ongar, who had denied her love for Harry Clavering to marry for money, and Florence Burton, who is too good to sacrifice the love ideal for money and is therefore content to undergo a long engagement to Harry before marriage. The theme is replayed with variations among minor characters like Sophie Gordeloup, who is villainous and mercenary, or Fanny Clavering, who learns to love Mr. Saul despite his poverty and is then rewarded with an income sufficient for marriage. The overt message—that one

should not sacrifice love for money—is reinforced not only by the
sharp contrast between Julia and Florence but also by judgments
within the narrative and statements made explicitly by the narrator.

The irony of Julia's story demonstrates both kinds of judgments.
If Julia had not betrayed her love for Harry by marrying Lord Ongar
for money, she would eventually have become a baroness because
Harry's cousins (the evil Sir Hugh Clavering and the ineffectual Ar-
chie Clavering) are drowned, thereby making Harry's father the baronet and Harry his heir. This convenient drowning reinforces the
notion that those who are not evil or mercenary will be rewarded (itself a rather inconsistent notion since money becomes the reward for
not wanting money). The same reinforcement is effected in the minor
plot of Fanny Clavering and Mr. Saul; since they are true to their love
in poverty, Mr. Saul is (by Hugh's death) awarded an income sufficient for marriage.

The narrator's judgments about Julia are similar: "She had disgraced herself, ruined herself, robbed herself of all happiness by the
marriage she had made. Her misery had not been simply the misery
of that lord's lifetime. . . . The very knowledge of her wealth was a
burden to her. And as she thought of her riches . . . she came to
understand that she was degraded by their acquisition. She had done
that which had been unpardonably bad, and she felt like Judas when
he stood with the price of his treachery in his hand" (42). By the end
of the novel, the plot, the narrator, and Julia herself all agree in judging her to have so sinned as to be unworthy of reward.

Nevertheless, the novel is not entirely straightforward because its
overt judgments conceal some ambivalence. Part of Julia's crime lies
in her use of sexual allure. Harry, unable to marry Florence without
a prolonged engagement, finds Julia's beauty and sexuality enticing,
and readers probably agree with Harry in finding Julia more interesting than the innocent but insipid Florence. When the novel's happy
ending is almost at hand, Harry's mother finds it necessary to urge
Florence to agree to a prompt marriage so that Harry will not be tempted again. At this point the narrator seems to be ridiculing Florence's squeamishness or lack of comprehension:

[Mrs. Clavering says,] "You see Harry is a young man of that sort,—so im-
petuous I mean, you know, and so eager,—and so—you know what I
mean,—that the sooner he is married the better." . . . Whether or no Mrs.
Clavering had present in her imagination the possibility of any further dam-

age that might result from Lady Ongar, I will not say, but if so, she altogether failed in communicating her idea to Florence.

Then I must go home at once," said Florence, driven almost to bewail the terrors of her position. (47)

Despite the overt approval of Florence present in both the plot and the narrator's comments, this scene certainly suggests that Trollope is not altogether uncritical of Florence's brand of innocent goodness.

A similar ambivalence enters into the portrayal of Mr. Saul and Fanny Clavering. About their engagement, Mrs. Clavering, her husband, and even the innocent Florence all express some disapproval. When Mr. Saul tells Mrs. Clavering that his newly enhanced income will make them too comfortable, Mrs. Clavering "could not but wonder at her daughter's taste." Mr. Clavering, observing Fanny's grave and silent demeanor, remarks, "There are to be no more cakes and ale in the parish." And even Florence reacts to Mr. Saul's asceticism by hoping "that a time might come, and that shortly, in which Mr. Saul might moderate his views" (48). In this way, the novel's overt approval of its most innocent characters is somewhat undercut.

The Claverings anticipates the deepening pessimism of Trollope's later novels through this ambiguity. Innocence is seen, not just as insipid, but also as impotent, while sexuality is treated more seriously than in earlier novels. In *Barchester Towers,* for instance, Mr. Slope's sexual ambitions are more comic than sinister while Signora Neroni's sirenlike charms are essentially comic and liberating, rather than threatening. But society is depicted in *The Claverings* far less comically. Julia Ongar's husband (whom she married for money) is shown as sadomasochistic while her brother-in-law, Hugh Clavering, acts as sadist to his masochistic wife, Hermione, in a sort of marital master-slave relationship. Both Ongar and Hugh Clavering are far more sinister than Mr. Slope, while Julia's sexuality is far more humanized and alluring than Madeline Neroni's and the innocent heroine far more impotent than Eleanor Bold. *The Claverings* may thus be viewed as an important early work anticipating similar explorations of love and money in Trollope's later novels.

Phineas Finn (1869) and *Phineas Redux* (1874)

The two Phineas novels, when viewed together, illustrate Trollope's growing pessimism rather dramatically, and while the strength of his pessimism is directed at the ill effects of public upon private life, love and marriage do not escape his darkening vision.[4]

The parts of *Phineas Finn* and *Phineas Redux* that concern women and marriage are structured in several ways: (1) by the parallels between the political world of men and the social world of women (see chapter 6), (2) by the parallels and contrasts between the courtship plots of Laura and Violet, and (3) by Laura's growing inability to reconcile public and private worlds.

Lady Laura Kennedy and Violet Effingham in *Phineas Finn* are both wary about the roles of women in marriage, but they attempt different solutions. Violet complains about the lot of women and jokes openly about rebellion, staying single, or endorsing John Stuart Mill's feminist position. Her wariness is clearly warranted in relation to her suitor, the rather violent Lord Chiltern. Laura, by contrast, believes initially that she can accomplish whatever she wants by working through men; she does not appear rebellious, and the suitor she chooses, Robert Kennedy, appears to be Chiltern's opposite—gentlemanly, responsible, tractable, not violent. Though she feels she is being prudent, Laura's marrying Kennedy is actually rash because she does not love him. Violet, on the other hand, chooses the rash Chiltern only slowly and reluctantly, despite her love for him; hers is the true prudence. By *Phineas Redux* it is clear that the Chiltern marriage is a success, but the Kennedy marriage has proved disastrous to both Laura and Kennedy. They are living apart; Kennedy becomes mad and dies young, while Laura remains socially isolated and prematurely aged.

The reasons for Laura's failure are to be found in Trollope's development of the theme of public and private. Initially in *Phineas Finn,* Laura is excessive in valuing the public and ignoring the private dimension, but by *Phineas Redux,* the undervalued private dimension has come to obsess her to the point that she is selfish and neurotic. She is unable to get beyond an obsessive concern with her own emotions and is, consequently, denied access to a more public social life or to the political world she once so loved.

With Laura, Trollope presents another variation of the woman who marries for money. Unlike Lady Mason or Julia Ongar, Laura is more unwise than unprincipled. She begins with status and a fortune of her own, but turns her money over to her brother (Lord Chiltern) to pay his debts. In this decision, Laura resembles the women of *Can You Forgive Her?*—especially Kate and Alice Vavasor, both of whom try

to live vicariously through George Vavasor. These women suffer a
sense of diminishment because they live in a society that allows
women to act only through men.

Lady Laura in *Phineas Finn* wants to have political power, but she
is not a feminist; she does not protest against the lot of women, as
Violet occasionally does. Laura does not acknowledge her limits at
first; she sees marriage and the social sphere as means by which she
can vicariously experience political excitement. Though she is tempted to love Phineas at the beginning of the novel, she chooses not
to marry him because he lacks money and status. Instead she decides
to ignore her heart and marry a man with a political position and a
great deal of money, not realizing that she may later lament her decision. She feels that as Kennedy's wife she can indirectly influence
male political figures in their decision making and, as one consequence, continue to sponsor Phineas's political career. Her plan is upset, however, because her ability to control herself and to influence
her husband are destroyed when her love for Phineas grows uncontrol-
lably.

When she realizes how much she dislikes her husband's coldness,
religious severity, and domineering attitude, she indulges herself in
her feelings for Phineas, managing thereby in both Phineas novels to
harm her husband, Phineas, and herself through her self-indulgence.
By *Phineas Redux* when Phineas stands to lose access to political office
if scandal touches him, Laura's insistence upon her love for Phineas is
damaging, but she is more concerned with her own feelings than with
their effects upon others. In this way, she illustrates the danger of
both extremes—the extreme of marrying a man whom she does not
love (thereby ignoring her emotional needs) and the extreme of abandoning all responsibility other than indulgence in her private emotions.[5] The extreme of self-denial that she begins with appears to lead
naturally to a distortion of the inner life. Laura's difficulty in mediat-
ing between the public and private or outer and inner thereby mirrors
the trouble the male political figures have in balancing political and
private selves.

The Eustace Diamonds (1873)

Between the writing of *Phineas Finn,* which Trollope accomplished
in 1866–67, and *Phineas Redux,* in 1870–71, his pessimism was
fueled by his role in the Beverley election and his unsuccessful editor-

ship of *St. Paul's Magazine. The Eustace Diamonds,* written between the two Phineas novels, presents some of the earliest evidence of Trollope's increased disillusionment about the relation between public and private life.

The subjects of money and marriage appear in *The Eustace Diamonds,* once again connected to the theme of female innocence and guilt as well as the theme of lies versus truth. The novel includes two dominant courtship plots with two contrasted young women, Lizzie Eustace and Lucy Morris. Both are from the same class, connected by old family ties; both enter adulthood without money. Lizzie uses her beauty and her acting ability (or ability to deceive) to snare for herself a rich husband likely to die young. Sir Florian Eustace detects Lizzie's falsehoods about her jewelry, her debts, and her feelings before he dies, only months after their marriage. Lucy, by contrast, lacks Lizzie's external endowments—beauty and acting ability—but is said to be as good as gold. Lucy does not pursue an advantageous marriage and nearly loses her fiancé, Frank Greystock, because in his weakness he is tempted at times by Lizzie's money, beauty, and sirenlike charms. Thus the paired female characters provide a structure for the novel's two thematic contrasts: (1) marriage for money versus marriage for love and (2) lies versus truth.

A second structural device is the parallel between Lizzie's courtship plot and the plot concerning the thefts (and lies about) her diamonds. The two plots are thematically connected in several ways. First, even before her marriage to Sir Florian she has lied about some diamonds—using them to enhance her beauty in order to snare Sir Florian, lying to the dishonest jeweler (Mr. Benjamin), and forcing Sir Florian to pay her premarital expenses on the jewels. So from the beginning, the diamonds represent Lizzie's dishonesty, her preference for show over substance, and her desire to entrap men for mercenary reasons.

Once widowed, even though she is much better provided for than she had any right to be, Lizzie next appropriates the Eustace family diamonds. Her lies about Sir Florian's having given her the diamonds become increasingly clever until a number of people believe them, possibly even Lizzie herself; and the family lawyer, Mr. Camperdown, is utterly frustrated in his attempts to preserve the diamonds for the Eustace heir, Lizzie's own son.

Altogether there are five events involving both diamonds and lies: her premarital dealings, her appropriation of the family heirlooms, a theft at Carlisle, a second theft in London, and the trial of the thief

(Lizzie's jeweler Mr. Benjamin). In the Carlisle robbery, Lizzie hid the diamonds under her pillow, so only their box was stolen, and Lizzie perjured herself in order to keep the diamonds for herself. During a second robbery, they are truly stolen, and Lizzie faces the risk of detection after perjuring herself again. Finally, when the thieves are caught and tried, Lizzie has to testify and admit her previous perjury. Even so she manages to testify only at a hearing and then to lie that she is ill (even dying) in order to escape appearing at the trial.

Through these events Lizzie herself is depicted as having no inner self and therefore no true emotions. As a substitute for emotions, she likes romantic poetry (particularly Byron and Shelley)—or at least the appearance of liking poetry.[6] When accused of "lies" she is shaken, but when accused of providing "an incorrect version of the facts" (71), she feels quite comfortable, thereby demonstrating her almost exclusive concern for appearances. Similarly, at the end when Mr. Emilius proposes to her, she prefers his hyperbolic language to that of her other suitors, even though she knows he is both mercenary and deceitful:

She had never been made love to after this fashion before. She knew, or half knew, that the man was a scheming hypocrite, craving her money, and following her in the hour of her troubles, because he might then have the best chance of success. She had no belief whatever in his love. And yet she liked it, and approved his proceedings. She liked lies, thinking them to be more beautiful than truth. To lie readily and cleverly, recklessly and yet successfully, was, according to the lessons which she had learned, a necessity in woman, and an added grace in man. (79)

Lizzie thus in herself demonstrates a danger increasingly alarming to Trollope—the danger of preferring lies and dramatic display to truth or moral substance. She also acts as a touchstone by which other characters in the novel are revealed and judged.

The three suitors she plays with for most of the novel are very different from one another; Lord Fawn is stuffy and cowardly, Lord George is somewhat adventuresome and unconventional (Lizzie describes him as "Corsair-like"), and Franklin Greystock falls in between those two extremes. All three are drawn by Lizzie's money and beauty, but ultimately all three are appalled by her dishonesty and refuse to marry her. Only Mr. Emilius, who is as mercenary, deceitful, and hollow as Lizzie herself, is able or willing to marry her.

Among the minor characters the theme of lies versus truth appears also.[7] For instance, Miss MacNulty—Lizzie's plain, penniless, "humble, cowardly, and subservient" companion (6)—at times fails Lizzie, as the latter sees it, through refusing to lie. Whenever Lizzie tries to enlist Miss MacNulty's aid in perpetuating the fictions Lizzie lives by, Miss MacNulty is unswerving in her honesty. Fittingly, at the end when Lizzie tells of her own engagement to Emilius (whom Miss MacNulty herself had thought of loving) "Miss MacNulty was unable to answer a word" (79). Those who will not lie are almost left without the power of speech.

Lizzie's deficiencies are further underscored by two minor characters, Lucinda Roanoke and her aunt Mrs. Carbuncle, who, like Lizzie, pursue a mercenary marriage. Mrs. Carbuncle, without money of her own, wants to provide for her penniless but beautiful niece by getting her well married. Their motives are condemned, but Lucinda becomes interesting through her growing repulsion to the process. The three women (Lizzie, Mrs. Carbuncle, and Lucinda) "were worldly, hard, and given entirely to evil things. Even as regarded the bride, who felt the horror of her position, so much must be in truth admitted. Though from day to day and hour to hour she would openly declare her hatred of the things around her—yet she went on. Since she had entered upon life she had known nothing but falsehood and scheming wickedness;—and, though she rebelled against the consequences, she had not rebelled against the wickedness" (69). Lucinda thus belongs to the group of women like Lady Mason or Julia Ongar who, having once demeaned themselves, find it hard to change and who continue to have to pay for their sins. By her wedding day, Lucinda has been driven past the bounds of sanity. She refuses to leave her room; she is found with "a look of fixed but almost idiotic resolution," and she swears of her fiancé "he shall never touch me again alive" (70).

Before Lucinda reaches this point, however, we are entertained by Mrs. Carbuncle's efforts to secure for Lucinda wedding presents that may be turned into money. Mrs. Carbuncle's grasping parallels Lizzie's own appropriation of the Eustace diamonds, and Lizzie continues to act in character both by trying to reduce the amount of the gift she is forced to give Lucinda and by "assist[ing] the collection of tribute" so long as it does not come from her own purse (65). Their joint efforts are expended in writing letters to rather distant acquaintances virtually asking for wedding presents. At the end, when Lucinda refuses to marry, Mrs. Carbuncle is left "enveloped in a mass of debt which would have been hopeless, even had Lucinda gone off as a bride; but she had been willing to face all that with the object of establishing her niece" (70). In Mrs. Carbuncle, thus, we see again that women who prefer money to love in marriage are punished for their sins.

In this group of novels, the exaggerated comedy of Mrs. Carbuncle's grasping, the success Lizzie achieves with her lies, Lord Ongar's sexual perversity, Hugh Clavering's cruelty, and the extreme of Lady Mason's suffering are all signs of a shift within Trollope's realism. He continues to portray the everyday problems of rather ordinary people (like Lucy Morris, for instance), but he begins to include more extreme and excessive character traits in his examination of character. Whereas the quirks of a Mr. Slope or a Mrs. Proudie had once appeared sufficiently unthreatening to be treated comically in his early novels, characters like Lizzie Eustace are portrayed more seriously and present a greater threat to the good characters in the novel. Increasingly, his late novels are peopled with characters like Lizzie Eustace.

Chapter Five
Psychological Studies

In Trollope's novels from the mid-sixties onward may be found a new cluster of psychological concerns. The conflicts of the early novels were often external: Mary Throne's deciding whether to become engaged to Frank Gresham despite his parents' disapproval, Frank's need for money, Lucy Robarts's stance toward a lover whose mother disapproves of her. The more internal struggles—like Mr. Harding's decision to resign his wardenship or Mr. Palliser's decision not to accept a much coveted position because his wife needs him instead—involve both a strong moral element and a great degree of free choice. Both Harding and Palliser are free to examine their options and to decide upon either one.

By the mid-1860s, however, the internal struggles of Trollope's characters appear somewhat different: the struggles seem to belong to the domain of psychology more than morality, and there is a greater sense of internal compulsion involved in the choices characters make. The new cluster of concerns takes several forms: self-deception, indecision, self-destruction, paranoia, egotism, and even madness. These concerns are present among the novels of the mid-1860s discussed earlier; in Adolphus Crosbie (*Small House at Allington*), for instance, we see self-deception, indecision, and even self-destruction. Like Crosbie, Frank Greystock (*The Eustace Diamonds*) and Harry Clavering (*The Claverings*) also vacillate between young women, and several female characters (Alice Vavasor in *Can You Forgive Her?* and Clara Amedroz in *The Belton Estate*) vacillate between suitors. In George Vavasor's increasingly murderous state of mind (*Can You Forgive Her?*) we see self-destruction and paranoia that stop just short of madness, while in Lord Ongar and Sir Hugh Clavering (*The Claverings*) we see abuse of marital power.

With *The Last Chronicle of Barset* (1867) and *He Knew He Was Right* (1869) Trollope's exploration of similar psychological phenomena becomes more thorough and intense, with a more subtle depiction of the interrelation between personality and environment.

The Last Chronicle of Barset (1867)

The portrait of the Reverend Josiah Crawley in *The Last Chronicle of Barset* provides some of Trollope's richest insights into how a man may be driven by conflicting internal and external pressures—a man, in Crawley's case, very like Trollope's own father.

Modern psychologists could find, in Trollope's depiction of Crawley, support for the theory that "personality" is the result of interaction between traits inherent in the person and external situations or the general cultural environment. When Crawley is accused of stealing a check for twenty pounds and is unable to explain where he got it, all Barchester comes to believe either that he is guilty or, more commonly, that he is innocent because he is mad. Contributing to the situation are a number of internal and external factors.

To begin with, Crawley is given to depression. He is a scholar who knows Greek, Latin, and Hebrew and would have his children console themselves in affliction by reading Greek. He seems predisposed to take a gloomy view of things and is altogether incapable of adopting the cheerful openness (and occasional vulgarity) of the London lawyer Mr. Toogood. Even in prosperity, Crawley would probably have tended to gloom, but prosperity would have made it less marked. Under the threat of both poverty and disgrace, however, Crawley's depression dominates his personality.

He is also proud and would have been so in other circumstances, though possibly pride and depression help to prevent him from being more fortunate. His pride, complicated by reticence and social uneasiness, is of the sort that refuses to accept pity, charity, or even sympathy from those who are more fortunate. He could readily gain sympathy from Archdeacon Grantly, Lady Lufton, and the other Barchester anti-Proudieites who cement their social solidarity through having Mrs. Proudie to abuse. But even though Crawley inwardly glories in crushing the bishop and Mrs. Proudie, he refuses to court or accept social approval for doing so. When he is summoned by the bishop, Crawley takes great pride in humbling himself—walking through the thick of the mud on the way to Barchester to demonstrate his poverty as dramatically as possible, all the while congratulating himself for his humility.

He behaves with the same ostentatious humility with Mr. Robarts; though Robarts is an anti-Proudieite and sympathizer with Crawley, the latter cannot forgive Robarts for finding life so easy. When Robarts goes to Crawley's house to urge him to hire a lawyer and to offer the help of Archdeacon Grantly, Crawley adopts an apologetic air: "And, even in his own house, Mr. Crawley affected a mock humility, as though, either through his own debasement, or because of the superior station of the other clergyman, he were not entitled to put himself on an equal footing with his visitor" (21). Robarts understands Crawley, knowing "that behind the humility there was a crushing pride,—a pride which, in all probability, would rise up and crush him before he could get himself out of the room again." And then when Robarts ventures to empathize with Crawley by suggesting that Grantly and Crawley are on the same side in disliking the bishop, Crawley repulses Robarts's attempt by saying, "I by no means wish to derogate from Dr. Grantly's high position in his own archdeaconry . . . nor to criticize his conduct in any respect. . . .But I cannot accept it as a point in a clergyman's favour, that he should be opposed to his bishop" (21). Knowing of Crawley's own opposition to the bishop, Robarts is somewhat incredulous, but Crawley is so determined to argue with potential sympathizers who are more fortunate than he, that Robarts can do nothing with him.

This complicated form of pride, then, also becomes a rather devious tool for asserting power over others or maintaining his superiority and isolation in social encounters. Because of Crawley's poverty and threatened disgrace, this kind of desire for power—spurning sympathy and asserting himself independently when he is so greatly in need—strikes others as mad. If madness here is equated with self-destructiveness, certainly most of Crawley's actions are mad because he constantly refuses the kind of help that he and his family seem to need.

Another personality trait that contributes to Crawley's dilemma is a truer kind of humility. Despite his initial error in saying that Soames gave him the check, Crawley then recalls getting the check from Dean Arabin—as it eventually is proved that he did. But when the dean says the check did not come from him (Arabin's wife having included the check without telling her husband), everyone, including Crawley himself, believes Arabin's rather than Crawley's version of the facts. Much of Crawley's torment and much of the community's sense that he is unfit for his position comes from the sense that a man with a memory so faulty must be mad. In reality, Crawley's memory is hardly faulty at all. What is interesting is his and the community's readiness to believe that he must be mad. In the end, Crawley's false pride is somewhat forgiven because of his true humility in being willing to think himself mad rather than think that Arabin could be mistaken:

> So far have I been from misdoubting the dean . . . that I postponed the elaborated result of my own memory to his word. And I felt myself the more constrained to do this because, in a moment of forgetfulness, in the wantonness of inconsiderate haste, with wicked thoughtlessness, I had allowed myself to make a false statement,—unwittingly false, indeed, nathless very false, unpardonably false. . . . When I had been guilty of so great a blunder . . . how could I expect that any one should accept my statement when contravened by that made by the dean? How, in such an embarrassment, could I believe my own memory? (74)

Major Crawley and Mr. Toogood have tears in their eyes after this speech. Their reactions are summed up by Toogood: "I never heard such a thing in all my life . . . to find a man who was going to let everything in the world go against him, because he believed another fellow better than himself! . . . It's not natural; and the world wouldn't go on if there were many like that" (74). Toogood's reaction illuminates another dimension of the novel—the contrast between the unworldly thinking of Mr. Crawley and the too worldly thinking of the rest of his society, and therefore the difficulty Mr. Crawley experiences in acting like other people.

The often criticized London sections of the novel show by contrast the creeping materialism and characterlessness of the society around Crawley.[1] False, empty, or scheming women (Mrs. Dobbs Broughton, Madalina Demolines); a speculator who commits suicide (Dobbs Broughton); a painter who paints society women for money; the older, debt-ridden, more tawdry Adolphus Crosbie, John Eames's false and bragging superior (Sir Raffle Buffle)—the characters of the London scenes show an emptiness of character and a materialistic accommodation foreign to Mr. Crawley. They are consistently described as playing games or acting. They are like Lizzie Eustace in having no self other than the poses they act out.

But the extremes of London are present to a lesser degree in characters who live in Barchester or characters (like John Eames and Mr. Toogood) who operate in both worlds. When refused by Lily Dale, John allows himself to fall into flirtation with the false and husband-hunting Madalina Demolines. Mr. Toogood—for all his goodness and sympathy for Mr. Crawley—is essentially incapable of understanding Crawley's strengths ("It's not natural," he said of Crawley, chap. 74). Mark Robarts's inability to make Crawley more tractable is a reminder of Robarts's own almost excessive flexibility—and the ethical dilemma it led him into in *Framley Parsonage*. Mrs. Crawley understands and loves her husband but is still to a degree unable to appreciate him; she is too worn down by mundane needs—the need for food and clothing for her family. Any number of minor characters are willing to accept and excuse Crawley for the theft they believe he has committed, but they are unable to see, as Crawley does, that such theft would be inexcusable except in the case of madness.

One of the episodes that dramatizes Crawley's difference from others is his resigning his ministry because he does not think a man accused as he is should remain as a minister and because he has learned from a brickmaker the importance of self-abnegation. But when Crawley submits his resignation to Dr. Tempest, the latter says Crawley's actions are "wicked" because the jury may yet acquit him. When Crawley replies that he cares nothing for the verdict, Dr. Tempest exclaims, "And you will turn your wife into the poorhouse for an idea!" (61). Tempest says Crawley has no right to resign as "an indulgence to [his] pride" when he has a wife and family (62). Tempest thus illustrates the pragmatic position in a conflict similar to that between Crawley and his wife over whether to accept charity. Tempest, Mrs. Crawley, Toogood, and Robarts all would urge Crawley to do what is necessary for his family, but such pragmatism is part of what Crawley rejects in his society—even at the cost of self-destruction.

Crawley wants to act upon principle—not simply from practical necessity—and he wants to be allowed the dignity of suffering for his principles. Immediately after the scene with Tempest, Crawley turns to reading Greek with his daughter and says, "Great power reduced to impotence, great glory to misery, by the hand of Fate,—Necessity, as the Greeks called her; the goddess that will not be shunned! . . . Polyphemus and Belisarius, and Samson and Milton, have always been pets of mine. The mind of the strong blind creature must be so sensible of the injury that has been done to him! The impotency, combined with his strength, or rather the impotency with the memory of former strength and former aspirations, is so essentially tragic!" (62). It is possible to interpret Crawley's stance as tragic or heroic in a society so unprincipled and so materialistic that it considers tragic suffering to be mad.[2] By this interpretation, both the death of Mr. Harding and the misunderstanding and scorn with which Crawley's attempts at heroism are met signify the passing of an age in which spiritual or moral heroism was possible.

Another possibility, however, is to see Crawley as self-destructive, as unnaturally heedless of the welfare of his family, and perhaps therefore as in need of integration into society for the sake of a happy or comic ending.[3] Whichever of these interpretations (or variants upon them) we adopt, however, we can see the intensity of Trollope's interest in the interactions between character and environment. We are free to judge Crawley's indisposition to act like others as pathological or self-destructive or heroic, but in any case we can see Trollope's fascination with the character whose internal compulsions force him to act against the norms of his society.

He Knew He Was Right (1869)

One difficulty of trying to assess Crawley's virtues and faults arises from his being alone of his kind in *The Last Chronicle*. In *He Knew He Was Right,* Trollope again undertakes a study of an obsessive, and in this case mad, man, but he uses the multiple plot structure to create ethical and psychological norms by which we may judge the protagonist's sanity.

The title of *He Knew He Was Right* provides, in its use of the word *right,* a clue for understanding Trollope's shift in emphasis from morality to psychology during this period. The increasingly mad Louis Trevelyan, to whom the title refers, is not the only character who is concerned with being right, and being "right" may mean one of three things. To begin with, it may be a matter of ethics and therefore concern such questions as whether it is right to deceive one's husband, cast off one's wife, or disinherit one's relations. In such contexts, right is conceived as a duty that is good for its own sake and separable from self-interest or the conscious and unconscious desires, needs, prejudices, or shortcomings of the people involved.

Some critics have felt that Trollope departs from all abstract or absolute traditional ethical thinking because he examines his characters' morality in context, in specific situations.[4] It is probably more accurate to argue, as James Kincaid has done, that Trollope uses context and situation to test morality, not to define it, and that despite the ambiguities of his novels, despite their attack on the abstract condemnations of rigid characters, there remain for Trollope ethical standards that are not simply relativistic.[5]

Nevertheless, the concept of right in *He Knew He Was Right* is for many of the characters woefully entangled with another sense of the word *right*—their rights. Right becomes, for some, dangerously obscured by their own obstinacy, their desire to be in the right, to have power over others. Obstinacy is a major theme of the novel in that Trevelyan, Emily, Nora, Hugh, Priscilla, and Miss Stanbury are all portrayed as characters who decidedly like their own way. When Trevelyan writes to Emily, "As I have done, and am doing what I think to be right, I cannot stultify myself by saying that I think I have been wrong" (5), the reader is able to see how the notion of abstract right or duty may be tainted by a person's desire to be right—to have his or her own way.

This second sense of *right* reveals a third sense: the question of right in this novel is also connected to the question of truth or correctness—the question of whether a character's interpretation of events is correct. So Trevelyan, in talking about what is morally right, demonstrates his psychological need to be right (to have his own way) and in the process is unable to perceive events or assess "facts" correctly. Thus there are two obstacles that prevent characters from acting in ways that are morally right: (1) the desire to have their own way at the expense of others and (2) the inability to perceive matters correctly without self-deception. These two failings occur in a number of the characters, with their fortunes in the novel directly related to their success at avoiding such lapses.

Most of the major characters have a strong streak of obstinacy. Trevelyan begins the novel with every possible endowment and the ability to be generous, but as he is tested by circumstances we discover the element of self-gratification in his generosity; he likes to patronize but cannot bear to be in a position of weakness or to be forgiven by an inferior like his wife. His wife, Emily, is equally self-willed—willing to forgive but not to be forgiven. In the end of the novel when Trevelyan is mad and dying, the narrator tells us, "All feeling of anger was over with her now. There is nothing that a woman will not forgive a man, when he is weaker than she is herself" (113). Emily and Trevelyan's willingness to patronize but not be patronized and Mr. Crawley's unwillingness to receive the sympathy of his friends have common roots in a love of power.

In numerous instances, Emily chafes against the restrictions and ultimatums laid down by her husband, then agrees to his commands in a legalistic rather than sympathetic way—agreeing only to do exactly as he has commanded, even when his commands imperfectly mirror his desires. She then triumphs by making her obedience just as distasteful to him as her rebellion.[6] The narrator sums up one such instance as follows:

In the matter of the quarrel, as it had hitherto progressed, the husband had perhaps been more in the wrong than his wife; but the wife, in spite of all her promises of perfect obedience, had proved herself to be a woman very hard to manage. Had she been earnest in her desire to please her lord and master in this matter of Colonel Osborne's visits,—to please him even after he had so vacillated in his own behests,—she might probably have so received the man as to have quelled all feeling of jealousy in her husband's bosom. But instead of doing so she had told herself that as she was innocent, and as her innocence had been acknowledged, and as she had been specially instructed to receive this man whom she had before been specially instructed not to receive, she would now fall back exactly into her old manner with him. (9)

Readers are able to judge Emily wrong not simply through comments from the narrator, but through comments from other characters who are sympathetic to her and devoid of Trevelyan's jealousy and paranoia. During one quarrel between Emily and Trevelyan, Nora exclaims, "How can you say such things,—on purpose to provoke him?" (6). Lady Millborough says elsewhere to Emily, "My dear, how could you bring yourself to use the word spy to your husband?" (11). And Priscilla says, "All that is twopenny-halfpenny pride, which should be thrown to the winds. The more right you have been hitherto the better you can afford to go on being right" (16).

The characters' obstinacy—their liking their own way—occurs, then, on a continuum. At the farthest extreme is the mad Louis Trevelyan who wants even the facts themselves to be bent to his desires. Emily is the second most extreme in obstinacy. At the other end of the continuum are the compliant characters—weak figures like Mrs. Stanbury or moderate ones like Dorothy Stanbury, who is both obliging and strong. In between are Nora Rowley, Hugh Stanbury, Miss Jemima Stanbury, and Priscilla Stanbury—all characters who are very strong-willed, yet too just, flexible, or truthful to go to the extreme of obstinacy seen in Trevelyan and his wife.

In the early quarrels between Trevelyan and Emily, Nora usually supports Emily (her sister) but urges her to be more moderate and to compromise for the sake of marital harmony. Yet in her own courtship by Hugh Stanbury, Nora shows the same kind of strong will that Emily has. The difference between them is that Emily hurts herself and others by her obstinacy whereas Nora hurts no one. Trollope's multiple plot structure is admirably suited to creating such distinctions. When Nora's father tries to intimidate Nora into obedience, he finds her just as intractable as Trevelyan found Emily in parallel circumstances. Sir Marmaduke Rowley's forbidding Nora to see Hugh or correspond with him resembles Trevelyan's forbidding Emily earlier to see or correspond with Colonel Osborne (70), and Nora's defying her father resembles Emily's defying Trevelyan. The difference between them is that Nora is more straightforward and less devious than Emily in her disobedience and it hurts no one.

For her combination of strength of character and honesty, Nora is a fitting wife for Hugh Stanbury, who shares those qualities. Hugh's tendency toward obstinacy is apparent in his quarrel with his aunt Miss Stanbury, but he is both more flexible and more honest than Trevelyan. When Trevelyan complains of Emily to Hugh, the latter replies that women do not like being "looked after" or told about their duties (19). Though Hugh is strong-willed enough almost to enjoy opposition from Nora's father (71), he is too truthful to distort events. He is capable of telling the truth unequivocally to Osborne, Trevelyan, and Bozzle.

Miss Stanbury resembles her nephew in being strong-willed, and at first she appears to be a self-deceived character, one of the many characters who believe what they want to believe and will bend the truth in order to have their own way. But despite her obstinacy; she has the Stanbury love of truth and is compelled by her own honesty to admit that she is wrong about several events. The first of these admissions comes when she has written to scold Priscilla and her mother for allowing Colonel Osborne to visit Emily Trevelyan while Emily is staying with the Stanburys. The gossip that has reached Miss Stanbury about a male visitor to the Stanburys is incorrect, and Priscilla with great "triumph" writes to tell her aunt that she has been wrong (18). Upon receiving her letter, Miss Stanbury turns "at first pale with dismay, and then red with renewed vigour and obstinacy" but she takes the trouble to discover that Priscilla has written the truth and then feels it necessary to apologize to Priscilla and her mother.

Eventually Colonel Osborne does visit Emily at the Stanbury home, however, and Emily is too foolish or too obstinate to refuse to see him. So it becomes Priscilla's turn to humble herself to her aunt. Neither aunt nor niece likes to admit she is wrong, but they are both too truthful to allow their desire for triumph to distort the truth. When Miss Stanbury received Priscilla's apology, she at first felt "triumph," but gradually "began to understand something of Priscilla's honesty, and began also to perceive that there might have been a great difficulty respecting the Colonel, for which neither her niece nor her sister-in-law could fairly be held to be responsible. It was perhaps the plainest characteristic of all the Stanburys that they were never wilfully dishonest. Ignorant, prejudiced, and passionate they might be. . . . But neither of them [Priscilla or her aunt] could lie,—even by silence" (22). And so Miss Stanbury "found herself compelled to acknowledge [the truth] aloud" (22).

Miss Stanbury has some of the traits that lead Trevelyan to his destruction, but her truthfulness and her warm heart preserve her from his fate. She has the same desire to wield power by generosity that we find in Trevelyan. When she attempts generosity toward Dorothy, she expects to be rewarded but does not expect the dependent Dorothy to have a will of her own: "She knew that she was going to behave with great generosity; that she was going to sacrifice, not her money only . . . but a considerable portion of her authority . . . and that she was about to behave in a manner which demanded much gratitude. But it seemed to her that Dorothy was not in the least grateful" (31). Miss Stanbury had already accused Hugh and the Burgess family of ingratitude, but she had not expected the mild-mannered Dorothy to deny her authority. After Dorothy refuses to marry Mr. Gibson (the suitor her aunt has chosen for her) and has received an offer of marriage from Brooke Burgess (Miss Stanbury's heir), the disagreement between aunt and niece reaches the point where Dorothy leaves Miss Stanbury to return to her mother and sister—just as Emily had left Trevelyan after their quarrel and secluded herself with the Stanbury ladies. But unlike Trevelyan, who hardens in his position, Miss Stanbury cannot bear Dorothy's absence and woos her to come back again, finally sanctioning the marriage between Dorothy and Brooke Burgess.

Throughout, Miss Stanbury is most "right" when she feels wrong, most "right" when she is most heedless of her own "rights." As the narrator tells us, "There was ever present to her mind an idea of failure and a fear lest she had been mistaken in her views throughout her life. No one had ever been more devoted to peculiar opinions, or more strong in the use of language for their expression; and she was so far true to herself, that she would never seem to retreat from the position she had taken. . . . She had believed herself to be right, and would not, even now, tell herself that she had been wrong; but there were doubts" (89). When Miss Stanbury sets aside her lifelong prejudices for the sake of others' happiness (and thereby increases her own happiness), she provides a standard against which we may judge both Emily and Trevelyan.

Emily's relationship to Colonel Osborne provides a case study of self-deceit and spurious self-rationalization. Colonel Osborne, to begin with, vacillates between claiming that he is merely an old friend of Emily's father and enjoying the thrill of feeling wicked. He goes through an elaborate process of self-justification before making his disastrous visit to her after her banishment to the country. He tells himself that he must "follow up the matter" and that Emily is "a dear injured saint." He is too vain to want to stay in the role of aging, fatherly comforter, but he is also too cautious to want to commit himself (21). So finally he convinces himself that he really went down to the country to see the door of a church.

Emily's rationalizations are similarly self-serving and self-deceitful. At one point early in the quarrel, she wants to resolve matters because she is guiltily conscious of having a secret from her husband, but almost immediately afterwards when Nora cautions her against keeping secrets from Trevelyan, Emily says indignantly, "What do you mean by secret? There isn't any secret" (2). Similarly, when Osborne writes to say he will visit her in her banishment to the country, Emily's thoughts are full of contradictions. She tells herself, "There was no reason moral, social, or religious, why an old man, over fifty, who had known her all her life, should not write to her. But yet she could not say aloud before Mrs. Stanbury, and Priscilla, and her sister, that she had received a letter from Colonel Osborne" (20). Her self-deceit here is obvious; she has not known Osborne all her life, and if there is nothing wrong with his visit, she should not be hesitant about others' knowing of it. Furthermore, the narrator tells us, "There was in it something of excitement. And she painted the man to herself in brighter colours now than she had ever given to him in her former portraits. He cared for her. He was gracious to her. He appreciated her talents, her beauty, and her conduct. He knew that she deserved a treatment very different from that accorded to her by her husband" (20). So when Nora reacts to Osborne's letter by exclaiming "How very wrong!" Emily replies, "I don't see that it is wrong at all" (20). If Emily had the honesty about her own motives that Priscilla and Miss Stanbury have, she would be unable to react as she does.

Louis Trevelyan resembles Emily both in his self-deceit and his love of being right, but he is more extreme than she and for that reason becomes mad, his madness compounded by other factors. Like Emily and unlike Miss Stanbury, he believes what he wants to believe and what will "prove" him "right": "He had taught himself to believe that she had disgraced him; and, though this feeling of disgrace made him so wretched that he wished that he were dead, he would allow himself to make no attempt at questioning the correctness of his conviction. Though he were to be shipwrecked for ever, even that seemed to be preferable to supposing that he had been wrong" (27).

Louis differs from Emily, however, in that he is weaker than she, more given to self-pity, and less able to gauge the effects of his pronouncements upon others. Whereas Emily early in the novel sometimes goads him on purpose, he usually fails to realize how offensive he is being to her. After he writes her a rather harsh letter, we are told: "He hardly recognised the force of the language which he used when he told her that her conduct was disgraceful, and that she had disgraced his name. He was quite unable to look at the whole question between him and his wife from her point of view. He conceived it possible that such a woman as his wife should be told that her conduct would be watched, and that she should be threatened with the Divorce Court, with an effect that should, upon the whole be salutary" (27).

Trollope writes of Trevelyan's madness, "There is perhaps no great social question so imperfectly understood among us at the present day as that which refers to the line which divides sanity from insanity" (38). Trollope knew from observing his own father how difficult it might be to explain the causes of madness. In Trevelyan's case, however, there are social factors that seem to contribute to madness—his concepts of the male role and of female purity.

Trevelyan conceives of husbands as patriarchal, almost godlike creatures: "He had given her his heart, and his hand, and his house, and had asked for nothing in return but that he should be all in all to her—that he should be her one god upon earth. . . . He was her master, and she must know that he was her master" (5). Later when

their separation has been accepted by all as irreversible and Trevelyan
has grown mad, he still focuses on the issue of power and his status
as male. He fears "yield[ing]" to her, being "robbed of what he loved
better than his liberty,—his power as a man." He fears she will "get
the better of him" in "this contest between him and her;" he has desired "to achieve empire" and still wants others to concede he was
right (79). So he clings to his principle of male superiority despite its
cost to him—his failing physical health.

Behind what Trevelyan and Emily say, the issue between them often seems to be simply power—who shall be right. But at times, in
his madness, the issue for Trevelyan shifts to that of female innocence. In the beginning, Trevelyan argues that "it is the very purity
of her innocence which makes the danger" (3). This is a conventional,
if already rather old-fashioned, Victorian belief that an innocent
woman must be shielded from knowledge of evil and that in her innocence she may run the danger of not recognizing the evil in others.

But soon we see in Trevelyan's concern for Emily's purity a more
selfish vein of concern for his own reputation when he says, "the
slightest rumour on a woman's name is a load of infamy on her husband's shoulders. It was not enough for Caesar that his wife should
be true; it was necessary to Caesar that she should not even be sus-
pected" (5). This reaction may seem male chauvinistic and egotistical,
but it was still within the range of normal behavior for a man of
Trevelyan's circumstances.

As his madness develops, however, we begin to see a prurient side
to his concern. He begins, at times, to relish the thought of her
guilt, even when he disavows doing so. He relies more and more
upon Bozzle because Bozzle alone may be able to obtain the "evidence" that a saner Louis Trevelyan would have hoped never to obtain:

He came to believe everything; and, though he prayed fervently that his wife
might not be led astray, that she might be saved at any rate from utter vice,
yet he almost came to hope that it might be otherwise;—not, indeed, with
the hope of the sane man, who desires that which he tells himself to be for
his advantage; but with the hope of the insane man, who loves to feed his
grievance, even though the grief should be his death. They who do not understand that a man may be brought to hope that which of all things is the
most grievous to him, have not observed with sufficient closeness the perversity of the human mind. (38)

Later when he tells Emily's mother that Emily must be "penitent" and "crushed in spirit" in order to become pure and happy again, we see how the issues of his power and her purity have become connected for him (62).

We see in Trevelyan, then, an element of extreme irrationality present in none of the other characters, even though his concern for power is reflected in them. Together the characters may be ranged on a continuum so that we see the self-destructive, obsessive nature of Trevelyan's thinking at the same time that more moderate characters like Hugh, Nora, or Miss Stanbury provide a standard by which to judge him. Their moderation, their willingness to give up their "rights" at times, their concern for truth and not simply vindication provide the standard of ethical behavior and sanity by which we may measure Trevelyan's departure from sanity.

In *The Last Chronicle of Barset* and *He Knew He Was Right,* Trollope creates his fullest psychological studies. The ethical dilemmas of the characters are rooted in social circumstances and influenced by variables in the characters' temperaments. Thus Trollope shows the complex interaction of temperament and social environment upon ethical decisions.

Chapter Six
The Social, Political, and Economic Dimension

In the late 1860s and continuing into the 1870s, Trollope increasingly explores problems associated with social, political, and economic change. The plots of his earlier novels often centered upon maintaining or restoring social and economic stasis. Social climbing, for instance, is treated comically through characters like Slope or the aptly-named Mrs. Lookaloft in *Barchester Towers*. In *Doctor Thorne* Mary is allowed to rise in class only because her manners and values are equal (or superior) to those of the family she would marry into and because her wealth will restore the Greshams to their place in society. In the early novels in general, Trollope deals with issues of social mobility only in limited ways—i.e., making an exception here and there for an exemplary character, finding comedy or even crime in inappropriate behavior. But the late 1860s brought associated social, political, and economic changes that increased social mobility while also decreasing the deference felt toward the older status quo.[1] What many consider Trollope's most brilliant and complex novels—*Phineas Finn* (1869), *Phineas Redux* (1874), *The Way We Live Now* (1875), *The Prime Minister* (1876), and *The Duke's Children* (1880)—all deal with politics, with the relation between the individual and public opinion, and with the socioeconomic changes in Victorian society of their decade.

In *Phineas Finn* Trollope depicts optimistically the rise of a young man rather different from his earlier heroes. Finn is an outsider (an Irishman), not from the upper classes (the son of a doctor), not independently wealthy (living on an allowance from his father of several hundred pounds a year), and not tied initially to any of the political families that could smooth his rise. Yet he succeeds in rising in life without the initial advantages of wealth, class, or influence; he gains a seat in Parliament, secures a government post, and becomes a viable contender for the hand of several young women who have wealth and status. He succeeds through good luck, a pleasing personality, and a reasonable degree of intelligence and hard work. Most important, he retains his integrity and in the end gives up what he has achieved (his government position, his seat in Parliament, and the possibility of marriage to a wealthy Londoner) rather than compromise his integrity.

Despite—perhaps even because of—his renunciation, we are left at the end of *Phineas Finn* with the impression that hard work and integrity will be appreciated, that good luck is more likely than bad luck, and that deserving young men can rise and be accommodated by the social and political system without undue strain upon it; even though Phineas feels forced to resign his position at the end, there is a sense that virtue has triumphed and that therefore the good can continue to prevail. Much of this optimism, however, disappears in the novels that follow *Phineas Finn*. Both Trollope's Victorian readers and critics today have sensed a change in tone in Trollope's novels at about this point; modern scholars often attribute the change to Trollope's disappointment at the Beverley election in 1868, the year after he finished writing *Phineas Finn*.[2]

The disillusion with the electoral process appears in *Ralph the Heir* (1871) with its account of the election corruption that Trollope suffered from at Beverley. But the sense of general disillusionment appears first and most strikingly, perhaps, in *The Eustace Diamonds* (1873), with its cynical view of Lizzie Eustace—a character devoid of all the virtues of Mary Thorne or Phineas Finn, yet able to rise socially in a society no longer capable of discriminating between good and bad or honest and dishonest. As we have seen, Trollope depicts in the grasping Lizzie Eustace a woman so enamored of lies that she loses the ability to see the truth or to distinguish between self and the image of self that she strives to project. Trollope's examination of Lizzie's lack of self in *The Eustace Diamonds* seems, in the interval between *Phineas Finn* and *Phineas Redux,* to have opened up for him new problems for exploration, some with more far-reaching implications than are immediately apparent in *The Eustace Diamonds* itself. In *Phineas Redux, The Way We Live Now,* and *The Prime Minister,* Trollope takes up the consequences of social, political, and economic mobility; he explores how traditional characters (like Mr. Palliser) and some adventurers akin to Lizzie Eustace fare in a changing England. He examines the relation between the public realm and the private one as well as the relation between the political and the social world. And what he sees in England of the 1870s is disturbing enough to him that he modifies the nature of his realism—including more extreme, symbolic, or melodramatic elements in his realistic portrayals in order to depict what he sees as increasingly extreme and dangerous tendencies in his society.

Phineas Redux (1874)

A number of conflicts between self-interest and integrity are associated with Phineas's rise in the political and social world of *Phineas Redux*. Having chosen integrity rather than self-interest at the end of *Phineas Finn*, Phineas returns to London several years later and finds that self-interest has distorted the nature of the political process. Already in *Phineas Finn* he had discovered several flaws in the political system. First of all, a man without money, like Phineas, needed to find a government position, but such positions were only given to loyal party followers. Once he has a position in the government, Phineas feels a great deal of pressure to endorse the party position, despite his individual convictions. He also finds that do-nothing party loyalists (like Laurence Fitzgibbon) are often valued more highly than someone (like himself) who takes his work and the issues seriously. In *Phineas Redux* the proportion of serious concern for issues is seen to dwindle while opportunism appears to be on the rise.

The prime minister, as the novel opens, is Mr. Daubeny, a character modeled upon a prime minister of the day, Benjamin Disraeli, whom Trollope disliked and distrusted. In order to keep power without a majority, Daubeny has seized upon the issue of Church Disestablishment. Trollope's purpose being to satirize Disraeli rather than to depict the actual issues of the day, he uses artistic license to heighten the opportunism he accuses Disraeli of.[3] Disraeli, as a Tory (conservative), leads the party most likely to want to preserve the strength of the established church, so Trollope satirizes Disraeli and his party by depicting them as willing to violate their most cherished beliefs in order to maintain political power. In *Phineas Redux*, Daubeny, Disraeli's fictional counterpart, hopes by bringing up the issue of Church Disestablishment, to gain enough support from three groups to be able to retain power. First, the conservatives in his own party who favor the church will nevertheless support the measure, though they hate it, in order to retain power.

Second, many conservatives and liberals alike will support it because Daubeny threatens to dissolve Parliament if he is defeated; they fear a new election will cost too much or may bring their defeat. Finally, some liberals or radicals will support it because they approve of the measure itself. Liberals who follow the party line are therefore forced to vote against their own convictions if they wish to regain power, so Trollope treats us to the spectacle of almost everyone, no matter what his political beliefs, voting against those beliefs out of self-interest. Private beliefs have become virtually irrelevant to the public presentation of self in the political realm.

One of the main mischief-makers of *Phineas Redux,* the editor of the *People's Banner,* Quintus Slide, also demonstrates how self-interest overcomes integrity. Already offended by Phineas in *Phineas Finn,* Slide is further aggrieved in *Phineas Redux;* he obtains a letter Mr. Kennedy has written in his madness about Lady Laura's deserting him. When Phineas urges Slide not to print a libelous letter because it is mad and concerns only private matters, Slide argues (with more self-deception than hypocrisy) that printing Kennedy's letter will serve the public by reinforcing the "purity of morals" (22). In lieu of self-knowledge or honesty, Slide resorts to heavy-handed rhetoric in order to manipulate public opinion. He says to Phineas, "Purity of morals, Finn;—punishment for the guilty;—defence for the innocent;—support for the weak;—safety for the oppressed;—and a rod of iron for the oppressors!" (22). It is no coincidence that the murderer Mr. Emilius uses similarly overblown and hypocritical language when trying to get money from Lizzie Eustace or when protesting his innocence (59); language has also become a means of manipulation rather than honest expression.

The issue of self-interest versus integrity thus is related to the issue of masks, deceit, or even the inability to judge others correctly: those who have no integrity create illusions and those who are too weak to judge for themselves are taken in by the illusions and swayed by the capriciousness of public opinion. These issues arise in relation to office holding also, just as in *Phineas Finn.* In the earlier novel, when Phineas found office holding to be incompatible with independent thinking, he resigned. At the beginning of *Phineas Redux,* he is coaxed to return to London life and Parliament largely through the hope of regaining office, but he becomes disillusioned for several reasons. First of all, his conviction that it is demeaning to have to vote as his party votes rather than according to his beliefs is further strengthened in *Phineas Redux.* He also comes to feel that it is demeaning to need to hold office in order to have an income. When he is attacked by the malicious Slide, he is "especially hurt by the allusions to his own poverty" and the necessity of his seeking office (28). And finally, he is disturbed and then angered when he realizes how often men are awarded office for reasons other than ability or kept from office because of the vagaries of public opinion. In *Phineas Redux,* the gossip surrounding Phineas's relation to Lady Laura, the malice of Slide and Bonteen, and shifting public opinion together keep Phineas out of office initially. Then after he is tried for murder and acquitted, he is offered office largely because unstable public opinion has veered around to favoring Phineas because of his misfortunes.

Public opinion in *Phineas Redux,* therefore, has become as hollow and without substance as the lies Lizzie Eustace manufactures. Trollope's political beliefs contain a mixture of both liberalism and conservatism, but on the issue of public opinion he is decidedly conservative. He sees it not as intrinsic to democracy or as the result of many thoughtful individuals expressing considered beliefs; instead he views it as capricious and easily manipulable. This is made particularly apparent through the two trials in the novel—the trial of Browborough for political bribery and the trial of Phineas for murder. Browborough is a man unworthy of serving in Parliament. A "great, hulking, heavy, speechless fellow" (1), he has retained his seat in Parliament through bribing the electors of Tankerville—until Phineas challenges him and the reformed election laws cause Browborough to be unseated. But once the seat has been awarded to Phineas, everyone begins to feel sorry for Browborough and then to consider him a hero.

The unreliability of public opinion is further dramatized through the malice of Slide's version of the facts. The narrator comments, "The People's Banner, setting at defiance with an admirable audacity all the facts as given in the Commissioners' report, declared that there was not one tittle of evidence against Mr. Browborough, and hinted that the trial had been got up by the malign influence of that doer of all evil, Phineas Finn" (44). Others, less partisan than Slide, simply follow public whim: "The only man treated with severity [as a result of the bribery trial] was poor Phineas Finn, and luckily for himself he was not present. His qualifications as member of Parliament for Tankerville were somewhat roughly treated. Each witness there, when he was asked what candidate would probably be returned for Tankerville at the next election, readily answered that Mr. Browborough would certainly carry the seat" (44). Thus Trollope demonstrates how caprice and self-interest mold public opinion in such a way that an individual's public image may have no reality to it at all.

It can be no accident that Trollope chose Lizzie Eustace's husband, the "Reverend" Mr. Emilius, to be the real murderer of Mr. Bonteen. The hollow Lizzie, lover of lies, has chosen her male counterpart to marry, and when Bonteen is murdered, the public has a choice between believing Emilius or Phineas to be the murderer. Emilius is the epitome of evil in *Phineas Redux* because he is a cynical manipulator of others' illusions and because he murders two men out of self-interest.[4] Knowing he will lose money by Bonteen's efforts to prove Lizzie is not married to Emilius, Emilius first has a man poisoned and then kills Bonteen. Though Emilius's economic self-interest in having Bonteen dead is apparent to everyone, they are far readier to believe that Phineas, who combines integrity with an honest rashness, is the murderer. Trollope's deepening pessimism about the public's ability to discriminate between truth and falsehood or innocence and guilt is seen in the general public belief that Phineas is the murderer.

Phineas's trial and its surrounding events demonstrate, first, how shaky even his friends' image of him is. Some (Glencora, Chiltern, Laura) believe Phineas to be innocent largely because of their own partisanship, rather than any objective reflection about Phineas's character. Others (Palliser, Mr. Monk, and other political men) attempt to be judicious and objective but in doing so are guided by the externals of circumstantial evidence rather than by knowledge of Phineas's inner character. The narrator explains Monk's reaction, "Since the circumstances of the case had come to his knowledge, they had weighed upon his mind so as to sadden his whole life. But he was a man who could not make his reason subordinate to his feelings. If the evidence against his friend was strong enough to send his friend for trial, how should he dare to discredit the evidence because the man was his friend?" (61). Though the two sets of Phineas's friends react differently, neither group has been able to connect emotion to reason, and so both groups are in effect blind to considerations of Phineas's inner nature.

If we assume that private character is the foundation upon which public images should be built rather than the reverse, then Trollope is suggesting that his society has arrived at a very unhealthy condition in which public images are highly manipulable and capricious but nevertheless assume greater importance than the private.

The unreliability of public opinion is further evident during the trial in the attorney Chaffanbrass's treatment of witnesses. Trollope had used Chaffanbrass in *Orley Farm* to demonstrate how easily a jury (and the public) could be made to doubt an honest witness and there-

fore to sympathize with Lady Mason, despite her guilt. He uses Chaffanbrass for the same purpose in *Phineas Redux*. Much of the case
against Phineas depends upon evidence given by Lord Fawn, who is
described by the narrator as "thoroughly under the influence of his
conscience as to his conduct," convinced of "the sanctity of an oath,"
and "essentially a truth-speaking man, if only he knew how to speak
the truth" (62). But because Fawn is pompous and rather stupid,
Chaffanbrass is able to make him appear to be hostile or a liar:

These facts Mr. Chaffanbrass extracted from his witness,—not without an
appearance of unwillingness, which was produced, however, altogether by
the natural antagonism of the victim to his persecutor; for Mr. Chaffanbrass,
even when asking the simplest questions, in the simplest words, even when
abstaining from that sarcasm of tone under which witnesses were wont to feel
that they were being flayed alive, could so look at a man as to create an
antagonism which no witness could conceal. In asking a man his name, and
age, and calling, he could produce an impression that the man was unwilling
to tell anything, and that, therefore, the jury were entitled to regard his evidence with suspicion. (62)

Thus, despite Fawn's honestly believing he saw Phineas, the jury and
the audience believe Fawn to be lying; they perceive his character as
incorrectly as many of them perceive Phineas's. (In reality, Fawn saw
Emilius, not Phineas, but he honestly believes at first that he saw
Phineas.)

Public images, in this way, either distort or create the private self,
instead of being true reflections of the private. The public image of
Phineas is a very distorted one that threatens to destroy his private
life and alter his nature. During the period surrounding his trial, Phineas loses his former optimism about life and becomes deeply disillusioned about his friends. Even after his innocence is discovered, he
remains permanently altered; he is unable to go out into society
among people capable of believing him guilty, and he even begins to
act like the murderer—prowling the scene of the crime at night in a
furtive manner.

Phineas's trial resembles Browborough's in that initially many people excuse or approve of his having murdered Bonteen. Later when
his innocence is established, they feel he should be reelected to the
seat in Parliament that he has resigned. Just as he was disturbed by
Browborough's popularity at the trial for bribery, at his own trial
Phineas is disturbed first by the false image others have of him and
then by the renewed popularity he acquires simply as a result of not

having killed a man. As he explains, "The horror I feel at being stared at, as the man that was not—hung as a murderer, is stronger than I can describe; and I am well aware that I shall be talked to and made a wonder of on that ground. I am told that I am to be re-elected triumphantly at Tankerville without a penny of cost or the trouble of asking for a vote, simply because I didn't knock poor Mr. Bonteen on the head. This to me is abominable" (70).

Phineas's engagement to Madame Max Goesler at the end is fitting because Madame Max, almost alone among his friends, has avoided judging solely by emotion or solely by reason. She believes Phineas to be innocent but also knows, by her reason and her knowledge of his character, that he could not have murdered Bonteen. Unlike the partisan Glencora, who would willingly bribe a judge to procure Phineas's release, or the self-indulgent Laura, who thinks more of her own distress than of Phineas's, Madame Max knows that Phineas will be unhappy as long as others still suspect him, so she sets out, not just to procure his release, but to establish his innocence. Because she believes in him and his innocence both emotionally and rationally, Madame Max is able to uncover evidence that will help Phineas. She is, therefore, the appropriate woman for Phineas to marry.

Nevertheless, the ending of *Phineas Redux* does not resemble the conventional happy endings of the early novels. Phineas and Madame Max have come together, but theirs is almost a union of outsiders. Phineas declines Gresham's offer of a government position, rather than be a part of the system that increasingly distresses him. Madame Max has undergone her own disillusion in *Phineas Finn* (as seen in her relation to the old Duke of Omnium); moreover as the widow of an Austrian banker, she has always been something of an outsider to English society.[5] Whereas the marriages of earlier novels symbolize the resolution of the conflicts in those works, Phineas's marriage to Madame Max instead almost symbolizes the impossibility of satisfaction within the sociopolitical setting of their day. At the end of the novel, the reader is left with the impression that a private happiness may be found but that it will rarely be joined to public position.

The Secular Society: *The Way We Live Now* (1875)

The pessimistic tone seen in *Phineas Redux* can be seen even more dramatically in *The Way We Live Now*. Trollope's novels before 1875 contain criticism of the legal system, the operations of the marriage market, oppressive evangelical religion, political elections, and of such personal failings as greed, callousness, infidelity, rigidity, egotism, or self-deceit. But Trollope's most extensive, penetrating, and systematic criticism of his society occurs in *The Way We Live Now* (1875) and is made more inclusive through the use of analogous plots and situations that link the economic, social, political, intellectual, and religious spheres.[6]

The central thematic conflict occurs between a traditional system of values represented by Roger Carbury and the challenge to those values—the "way we live now"—posed most dramatically by Augustus Melmotte. In the economic sphere, Roger Carbury demonstrates the reliance of the older, landed class upon the enduring and self-renewing value of land; Roger is a gentleman with whom the narrator, at least initially, seems to identify. Melmotte, on the other hand, initially appears to be a villain—a representative of shoddy new financial practices that involve creating wealth out of manipulation of public opinion. In the old system, Trollope implies, wealth was created through a combination of inherent value (e.g., land) and work, but in Melmotte's world, swindling and manipulation are more important than productive work.

There is more involved here than one individual's evildoing, however, for Melmotte represents a newer economic order, which was the result of the industrial revolution and the growth of England's capitalist economy in the mid-nineteenth century. Melmotte is presented as threatening at first, not just because he is a vaguely shady foreigner (with suspicious, perhaps American or Jewish ancestry), but also because he demonstrates rather dramatically the possibilities for exploitation and manipulation in unregulated capitalist growth.[7]

Melmotte is able to make money from speculation without any involvement in production. The central get-rich-quick scheme in the novel is to float a company for creating a "South Central Pacific and Mexican" railway running from Salt Lake City through the southwestern United States and Mexico to Vera Cruz. But its promoters (Fisker and then Melmotte) seem "indifferent whether the railway should ever be constructed or not. It was clearly [Fisker's] idea that fortunes were to be made out of the concern before a spadeful of earth had been moved" (9). Paul Montague, one of the novel's upper-class young men, is drawn into the scheme and becomes "grievously anxious to be really at work, and would attend most inopportunely at the Company's offices" until Fisker stops Paul's "folly" (10). Clearly work is not, for Fisker, the preliminary to wealth, and the object that is to result in wealth is not the railway itself but shares in the railway: their "fortune was to be made, not by the construction of the railway, but by the floating of the railway shares" (10). One result shows up in their language: "the words [of their documents] had no reference at all to the future profits of the railway, or to the benefit which such means of communication would confer upon the world at large; but applied solely to the appetite for such stock as theirs, which might certainly be produced in the speculating world by a proper manipulation of the affairs" (9). Trollope here is critical of the nineteenth-century dawning of what is today called market research. Melmotte, as symbol of the unscrupulous financier, is concerned not with a product or its intrinsic value but with either giving the public what it wants or making it think it wants what he has to sell.

The intellectual parallel to Melmotte's speculative and fraudulent activities occurs in Lady Carbury's story. She wants to make a living through writing books, but she believes that "her end was to be obtained not by producing good books, but by inducing certain people to say that her books were good" (2). She attempts to charm three male editors into writing laudatory reviews that will promote her book sales, and in the process we see that she is not alone in her lack of integrity. One editor refuses to be swayed by her flattery—not because of his own integrity: he makes profits by printing acerbic commentary that appeals to the public's desire to think poorly of others. A second editor compromises his literary integrity because he is romantically attracted to Lady Carbury, and a third editor feels he must praise Lady Carbury's books so that she in turn will write complimentary reviews of his books: "He felt it to be hard upon him that he should be compelled, by the exigencies of his position, to descend so low in literature; but it did not occur to him to reflect that in fact he was not compelled, and that he was quite at liberty to break stones, or to starve honestly, if no other honest mode of carrying on his career was open to him. 'If I didn't, somebody else would,' he said to himself" (11). He justifies his actions, therefore, not by appeal to any objective, external, or traditional standards of integrity, but by appeal to what everyone else is doing.

The contrast between the old and new ways of making money also appears in the stories of the young men who congregate at the Beargarden to drink and gamble. There are five or six young men who come from the top of the social scale, the landed gentry, or the better classes, but who are all seeking money without having to work for it.

Lord Nidderdale is good-natured but idle and is being forced by his father to try to marry Marie Melmotte for her money. Miles Grendall is the impoverished son of an impoverished lord and (along with his father) sells his services to Melmotte; together they give Melmotte aristocratic contacts and submit to performing a variety of demeaning chores in return for Melmotte's money. Their inconsistent morality is illustrated in the incident in which Felix realizes Miles is cheating at cards but cannot convince anyone else to take a stand for honesty (it being too troublesome and embarrassing to do so). Yet when Melmotte's downfall is about to occur, Miles turns up his nose in aristocratic disdain toward the man who has been supporting him. Dolly Longestaffe is an idle young man from the landed class who drinks, eats, and gambles too much and whose only energy is expended in quarreling with his father or maneuvering to prevent Melmotte from cheating him. Dolly has the virtue of not believing in Melmotte, but it is a rather negative virtue. Of active virtues he has none. Lord Glasslough is a fairly unimportant young man of the same group who quarrels with everyone. The worst of the group is Sir Felix Carbury, of whom more will be said below.

Just as Melmotte makes his profits from speculation in railway shares rather than railway building, the young men at the Beargarden gamble rather than work for their money, and since they are not producing any new wealth (through work, for instance), they soon resort to passing worthless pieces of paper back and forth. Their IOUs thus become analogous to the railway shares, pieces of paper supposed to represent wealth but actually without value. Similarly the young men live on credit rather than pay their debts.

Just as the young men's gambling parallels Melmotte's economic manipulations, the sexual sphere also acts as counterpart to the economic sphere. In addition to gambling and speculating, several of the young men consider making their fortunes by marrying for money. Their female counterparts have similar options; they have the possibility of rising in society by their fathers' speculations or by marrying for money. Both Marie Melmotte and Georgiana Longestaffe are in the first category; Melmotte sees his money-making partially as a tool for raising his daughter in society by marriage and thereby raising himself. Mr. Longestaffe, significantly, has exceeded the income available through his estate and so turns to London and Melmotte for ways to augment his income that will be newer, easier, and faster than cutting back on expenses and doing without luxuries. Though he is a neighbor of Roger Carbury's, when Longestaffe turns over his daughter, his London house, and the Pickering estate to Melmotte, he demonstrates his symbolic commitment to Melmotte, rather than to the traditional values Roger Carbury represents.

Since it is clear to Georgiana that her father's efforts will not be sufficient to dower her or find a suitor for her, she adopts a form of Melmottism on her own by trying to marry for money with little regard for the character or social status of her suitor. Marie Melmotte rebels against her father also, but not because he is failing to find her a suitor. She simply wants to choose for herself. Neither Marie nor Georgiana, however, is able to decide wisely or successfully.

In choosing for herself, Marie selects the worst of the young men from the Beargarden—Sir Felix Carbury. He is as hollow a sham as Melmotte or the railway stock—with a beautiful exterior but no fortune to support his title, no principles, no loyalty or fidelity, no emotions, and no energy even to pursue Marie consistently. Felix's patronizing and egotistical attitude toward the possible engagement to Marie becomes clear when Melmotte objects to Felix's lack of income:

The bloated swindler, the vile City ruffian, was certainly taking a most ungenerous advantage of the young aspirant for wealth. . . . Was he [Felix] not a baronet, and a gentleman, and a very handsome fellow, and a man of the world who had been in a crack regiment? If this surfeited sponge of speculation, this crammed commercial cormorant, wanted more than that for his daughter, why could he not say so without asking disgusting questions such as these—questions which it was quite impossible that a gentleman should answer? Was it not sufficiently plain that any gentleman proposing to marry the daughter of such a man as Melmotte must do so under the stress of pecuniary embarrassment? Would it not be an understood bargain that as he provided the rank and position, she would provide the money? (23)

Felix's concept of gentlemanliness here consists of externals only (rank, position, appearance), not of any inner characteristics, and Marie, in choosing a man to marry, is incapable of seeing past the externals to the hollowness within.[8]

Georgiana Longestaffe's position is the opposite of Marie's in that Georgiana has rank and position without money, but she is as incapable as Marie of discerning inner virtues in a suitor. Georgiana has insufficient money, beauty, or youth with which to attract men of the right sort; she is like Felix in wanting to gain money and status through marriage. The narrator describes Georgiana's pathetically dwindling expectations: "She had meant, when she first started on her career, to have a lord; but lords are scarce. She was herself not very highly born, not very highly gifted, not very lovely, not very pleasant, and she had no fortune. She had long made up her mind that she could do without a lord, but that she must get a commoner of the proper sort. . . . But now the men of the right sort never came near her. The one object for which she had subjected herself to all this ignominy seemed to have vanished altogether in the distance" (32). So in looking outside her own social circle to find a man with money but less social status, she discovers Mr. Brehgert, who is described as "a fat, greasy man, good-looking in a certain degree, about fifty, with hair dyed black, and beard and mustache dyed a dark purple color" (60). He is Jewish, a successful financier associated commercially with Melmotte, and a widower with two children.

While Georgiana's parents react with bigotry to her engagement to a Jew, Georgiana, like the other Londoners of the novel, has ironically gone beyond prejudices because she has also gone beyond principles: "For herself she regarded the matter [of Brehgert's being Jewish] not at all, except as far as it might be regarded by the world in which she wished to live. She was herself above all personal prejudices of that kind. Jew, Turk, or infidel was nothing to her" (60).

The foolish and unprincipled quality of Georgiana's lack of prejudice is made most apparent at the crisis of her engagement to Brehgert, after her parents' disapproval is made clear. The now vacillating Georgiana receives a letter from Brehgert explaining that because of Melmotte's financial collapse Brehgert will be unable to keep a second house for two or three years. Since Georgiana has been interested in marrying Brehgert almost solely because of his money and his ability to establish her in London, none of the good sense or charity his letter shows has any effect on her: "She could understand that it was a plain-spoken and truth-telling letter. Not that she, to herself, gave it praise for those virtues. . . . But the single-minded, genuine honesty of the letter was altogether thrown away upon her" (79). Instead she is annoyed by a number of minor points (references to her age and the possibility of their having children) but especially by his loss of money and consequent inability to have a town house. After her demanding response and his subsequent withdrawal from their engagement, Georgiana still has learned nothing about Brehgert's intrinsic value as a man or about her own shortcomings.

In her disregard for Brehgert's inner qualities, Georgiana thus resembles the nobility (like the Grendalls) who lend their prestige to Melmotte without esteeming him, the men of the Beargarden who are too jaded to feel shocked at their friends' cheating or too lazy to do anything about it, the editors who write false reviews, and the public who admire Melmotte enough to buy his shares or to vote for him for Parliament. The marriage market, thus, in the case of both Marie and Georgiana demonstrates people operating with the same shallow principles and the same preference for appearance rather than worth that can be seen in the economic sphere.

The Way We Live Now, as is typical of other Trollope novels, appears to give mixed messages. Trollope's attachment to Roger Carbury may seem to demonstrate an old-fashioned conservatism, a preference for traditional England, and a denial of the democratic tendencies that allowed social mobility for such characters as Melmotte, Mrs. Hurtle, Lizzie Eustace, or, as we will see in *The Prime Minister,* Ferdinand Lopez. His treatment of Melmotte and the forms of Melmottism seen in Lady Carbury or the Beargarden men may then seem like a hopelessly old-fashioned reaction to the socioeconomic condition of his society. But his reaction may also be seen as perceptive and even farsighted; by comparison Dickens's satiric portrait of the capitalist Merdle in *Little Dorrit,* Robin Gilmour has argued, is one-dimensional.[9] Dickens had a way of simplifying issues and turning them into moral problems, but in *The Way We Live Now* Trollope does something more complex and more sociological. He shows how the socioeconomic environment has an influence upon individuals— how a man like Melmotte not only creates, but is created by his environment and how speculation, image manipulation, and lack of integrity were related phenomena at many different levels of his society.

The Prime Minister (1876)

The disillusionment pervading *Phineas Redux* and *The Way We Live Now* runs through *The Prime Minister* also. The discrepancy between private and public present in *Phineas Redux* appears in the Duke of Omnium (formerly Mr. Palliser) who becomes prime minister but never reconciles himself to the misinterpretations made of his actions. The contrast between integrity and self-interest present in *Phineas Redux* or that between intrinsic worth and speculation in *The Way We Live Now* informs the parallel plots of the prime minister and Ferdinand Lopez.

Just as Roger Carbury in *The Way We Live Now* stands stoutly but rather forlornly for a traditional system in which value is placed upon something of intrinsic worth—such as work or land—so in *The Prime Minister* the duke stands for older, more traditional values (such as work, service to one's country, protection of one's wife, honesty, and integrity) that are somewhat incompatible with the political, social, and economic trends of his day. The duke began his political life loving work, dedicated to studying blue books of facts, and tirelessly interested in converting to decimal coinage, but after his accession to dukedom in *Phineas Redux* he finds himself prevented from the useful work of the House of Commons by his new title and his seat in the House of Lords. He rises unwillingly once again in *The Prime Minister,* only to find himself further prevented from useful work. Men beneath him are still allowed to work, but he sorrows to find himself confined to serving only as an image:

There were men under him who were really at work. The Lord Chancellor had legal reforms on foot. Mr. Monk was busy, heart and soul, in regard to income tax and brewers' licences,—making our poor Prime Minister's mouth water. Lord Drummond was active among the colonies. Phineas Finn had at any rate his ideas about Ireland. But with the Prime Minister . . . it was all a blank. The policy confided to him and expected at his hands was that of keeping together a Coalition Ministry. That was a task that did not satisfy him. And now, gradually . . . there was creeping upon him the idea that his power of cohesion was sought for, and perhaps found, not in his political capacity, but in his rank and wealth. It might, in fact, be the case that it was his wife the Duchess . . . with her dinner parties and receptions, with her crowded saloons, her music, her picnics, and social temptations, [who] was Prime Minister rather than he himself. (18)

At one point the duke laments the "absence of real work and the quantity of mock work" (27), and indeed there is a great deal of mock work surrounding him. In the political sphere, Sir Orlando Drought makes himself repugnant to the duke by suggesting that the coalition ministry the duke heads should have a policy. The duke shows his preference for work that has intrinsic value when he replies, "Things to be done offer themselves, I suppose, because they are in themselves desirable; not because it is desirable to have something to do" (20). But Sir Orlando continues to urge increased armaments, not for their own sake, but for the sake of having a policy.

In the social sphere, Glencora, now the Duchess of Omnium, finds her elevated position almost as difficult as her husband's. At first she is thrilled by her husband's position and attempts to help him by her social skills. She invites large groups of people to Gatherum Castle and spends large amounts of money on entertaining them, turning her family's private life upside down and nearly wearing herself out in the process—all in the hope of cementing the coalition around the duke because of her hospitality. At first she likes the work; after all, as a woman she has no other method of political work available to her than using the social sphere for political purposes. But eventually she discovers the emptiness of her activity just as the duke has discovered the emptiness of his. Some of her guests become offensive, others are insulted by not being invited, and in the end both Glencora and the duke feel that she has lowered herself—made herself "vulgar" the duke complains—by her activities, probably hurting her husband more than if she had kept herself and her home coolly aloof.

In one sense Glencora is contrasted to the duke because she has tried to solidify political power by a social sleight of hand unrelated to the work of government, but in another sense she is like her husband in that they both discover—he from his political pinnacle and she from her social one—the emptiness of their public positions.[10]

The sharpest contrast to the values the duke represents may be found in the parallel plot of Ferdinand Lopez, a speculator like Melmotte, who attempts to create wealth by sleight of hand almost without capital. Lopez is contrasted to the duke, who has honesty and nobility of character in conjunction with enormous land and wealth but is nevertheless frequently unappreciated or misunderstood. Lopez, however, at first contrives to make the best of appearances and is actually believed to have money even though he has none.

Lopez's manipulation of others' illusions puts him in a class with Trollope's other image-makers and manipulators (Melmotte, Quintus Slide, Lizzie Eustace, Mr. Emilius). He tries to cow his partner, Sexty Parker, into providing funds for their joint speculations, and then whenever Sexty becomes apprehensive, Lopez asserts himself and produces just enough money to calm Sexty's fears. Like Melmotte (who ran for Parliament in *The Way We Live Now*), Lopez tries running for Parliament because he sees political power as a route to monetary power. He knows that if he is believed to have money he will be in a better position to get money, and so at first he acts (like Melmotte) in such a way as to create a reputation without substance.

The antithesis between intrinsic value and speculation present in

The Way We Live Now occurs in a slightly different form in *The Prime Minister*, with speculation in commodities, rather than stock. Lopez explains his own philosophy when he contrasts himself to his father-in-law, Mr. Wharton, in the following exchange with Sexty Parker:

[Lopez says,] "I suppose old Wharton has been putting by two or three thousand out of his professional income, at any rate for the last thirty years, and never for a moment forgetting its natural increase. That's one way to make a fortune."

"It ain't rapid enough for you and me, Lopez."

"No. That was the old-fashioned way, and the most sure. But, as you say, it is not rapid enough; and it robs a man of the power of enjoying his money when he has made it." (30)

Lopez invests their capital (largely Sexty's capital) in coffee and guano, periodically allaying Sexty's fears, which "were greatly exaggerated by the feeling that the coffee and guano were not always real coffee and guano," by explaining that a speculator has no need of real coffee or guano and may even find them a hindrance (43)—much as Melmotte had no need of a real railway in order to cause the prices of railway shares to rise.

Lopez puts his money (what little he has) into forms of display: he exhibits power in order to bully Sexty; he flaunts his status by his wife's clothes and brougham. But then in private he forces economies upon his wife so long as they are not seen by the world (47). In this manner he resembles Trollope's other image-makers. Perhaps the most severe judgment is passed upon Lopez by Mrs. Parker, when Lopez is in the course of ruining her husband. She says Lopez and Sexty are "like tigers clawing one another. They don't care how many they kills, so that they has the least bit for themselves. There ain't no fear of God in it, nor yet no mercy, nor ere a morsel of heart. It ain't what I call manly,—not that longing after other folks' money. When it's come by hard work, as I tell Sexty,—by the very sweat of his brow,—oh,—it's sweet as sweet. . . . [Now] it's just as though he [Sexty] was a thirsting for blood" (47). Trollope almost certainly concurs in this judgment; he valued the money earned by hard work but passed judgment in horror at some of the speculation and illusion manipulation, as well as the marketing research mentality, that have come to be seen in the twentieth century as normal parts of a capitalist economic system. Trollope's sympathies were with more old-fashioned men like the Duke of Omnium who was antagonistic to borrowing (11) but committed to meaningful work.

As is so often characteristic of Trollope, there is some tension between his conservative, and at times self-complacent, criticism of parvenus and a deeper sympathy he feels for the lonely, the obsessed, and the driven. It can be argued that Trollope is biased in his treatment of Lopez in making one of the causes of Lopez's problems be that he is Jewish (a factor also for Melmotte, perhaps, as well as Disraeli and Emilius).[11] It can also be argued that in his disapproval of Lopez Trollope is making unfair demands of someone who begins life as an outsider—that an individual who starts off without upper-class family background, wealth, and sociopolitical influence will find it harder to achieve wealth, influence, or happiness and will therefore find it more difficult to act with the noble disinterestedness and integrity seen in the Duke of Omnium. But it should also be noted that despite Trollope's criticism of Lopez, he shows a great deal of sympathy in his portrait.[12] Readers who find Mr. Wharton's treatment of Lopez cruel are in effect responding to Trollope's insight into Wharton's cruelty, and if they find Lopez to be deserving of more sympathy, they are responding to a sympathy Trollope has induced them to feel. Despite Lopez's utter unscrupulousness, Trollope is able to make us feel his desperation—that of an outsider driven, sometimes against his better judgment, into an increasingly outrageous and self-destructive war upon those around him—his wife, his father-in-law, and his friends—who serve as substitutes in his frustrated desire to succeed.

Trollope knew at first hand (from his own early experiences and his father) how it felt to be the outsider, the obsessed, the self-destructive. In all three of these novels—*Phineas Redux, The Way We Live Now*, and *The Prime Minister*—Trollope creates outsiders whose initial acceptance and later rejection by society serve as touchstones to reveal the weaknesses of Victorian society.

Chapter Seven
The Perspective of Age

Perhaps the clue to understanding the late Tollope is to recognize, first of all, that many facets of the early Trollope remain unchanged— that the existence of a simple, conventional love plot with a happy ending may coexist with a significant thematic shift in the late novels. There indeed seems to have been such a shift, one that can be explained not by examining whether the endings are happy or not, but instead by the perspective from which events are viewed.

Some of the difficulty in defining the characteristics of the late novels may be illustrated with *Dr. Wortle's School* (1881). It has a marriage plot that is unique in Trollope's works; Mr. Peacock has married an American woman who appears to have been deserted and widowed by her first husband. Not long after their marriage, however, the first husband turns up alive after all but then disappears again. Peacock and his wife then return to England and continue to live as man and wife despite the illegality of their marriage. The moral questions raised by their living together, when the facts become known, are treated with enough ambiguity that Trollope readers are still not in agreement about whether Trollope applies a fixed standard of morality to the situation or whether he condones their living together and thereby advocates a situational ethics in which each case is judged on its own merits.[1] Since the same kind of debate exists about *The Warden*, we may conclude that Trollope's ethical stance is characteristically complex in both early and late novels. Yet in *Dr. Wortle's School,* the predicament of the Peacocks that raises the ethical questions is clearly one that later Victorians were able to confront in their literature far more comfortably than mid-Victorians could have done earlier. In this respect, then, *Dr. Wortle's School* provides evidence that Trollope's late novels were less conventional than his earlier ones.

Alongside the more open exploration of unconventional sexual relations in *Dr. Wortle's School,* however, is a conventional romance— scarcely fully developed—that could have appeared in any number of earlier Trollope novels. A young lord who attends Dr. Wortle's school falls in love with Mary Wortle. Mary and her parents worry that the young man's family will disdain the connection and be offended that Dr. Wortle could have allowed the situation to arise. All ends well, however, when the youth's father does not object to the match. This plot is certainly as optimistic as any similar plot in the early novels.

What separates the late novels from the early and middle ones is not so much theme or plot devices but the new focus within familiar themes and plots—the perspective of age and of the parent. In the *Autobiography* when Trollope wrote of the castles in the air he built as a boy he said, "I myself was of course my own hero" (p. 36). We may assume that even though a novelist like Trollope is able to create many hundreds of different characters—figures demonstrably not based upon his own life—he nevertheless projects himself into some of them and centers his novel upon their perspective. The early Trollope novels—like the majority of novels written in his day and earlier—are focused upon a young person of the age to undergo courtship. In *Tom Jones, Pamela, Pride and Prejudice, Jane Eyre,* or *Barchester Towers,* readers empathize with Tom, Pamela, Elizabeth Bennet, Jane Eyre, or Eleanor Bold rather than with Squire Allworthy, Pamela's parents, Mr. Bennet, Mrs. Fairfax, or Archdeacon Grantly, simply because the plot is constructed so that they shall do so.

The pattern is traditional to comedy in that young lovers are often blocked by well-meant but perhaps misdirected and overly conservative advice from their elders. From the start of his career Trollope was perhaps more generous in his depiction of elderly advisors than many other novelists have been; Mr. Harding and Dr. Thorne, for instance, are far wiser and more sympathetic characters than the Bennet parents or Lady Catherine in *Pride and Prejudice* or Nelly Dean in *Wuthering Heights.* But even so, the reader in Trollope's early novels empathizes with young characters going through courtship, undergoing apprenticeships, or engaged in a search for identity—Eleanor Bold; Mary Thorne and Frank Gresham; Lucy Robarts, Mark Robarts, and Lord Lufton; Rachel Ray and Luke Rowan; Glencora Palliser and Alice Vavasor; Phineas Finn and Lady Laura.

In Trollope's middle novels this focus begins to shift somewhat, particularly as Trollope develops his fascination with Plantagenet Palliser, who even in youth was more middle-aged than young. Virginia Woolf once said that George Eliot's *Middlemarch,* published in 1871 and 1872, was "one of the few English novels written for grown-up

people," but the same could be said of some of Trollope's novels written in the 1860s and later.[2] In the seventies in particular the point
of view of Trollope's novels shifts gradually from that of a young person entering the world to the concerns of those who are old enough
to sense the failure of their early aspirations. From the late seventies
until Trollope's death in 1882 the point of view shifts further toward
the concerns of the older generation looking on and indirectly participating, sometimes in hope and sometimes in agony, in the courtship
and apprenticeship of the young.

Is He Popenjoy? (1878)

Is He Popenjoy? illustrates the increased emphasis upon the parents'
perspective. In some respects the story of Mary Lovelace's marriage to
George Germain resembles the story of Glencora Palliser's marriage
in *Can You Forgive Her?* Both women marry without romance and
must learn to love their husbands while also negotiating some freedom for themselves within their marriages. Both novels derive their
happy ending from their heroines' giving birth to a child, symbol of
the success of the marriage. And both novels contain contradictions
on the subject of women's rights—overtly deriding women's rights
while at the same time creating sympathy for the problems women
and men face in marriage.[3]

Yet despite these similarities, *Is He Popenjoy?* differs from the earlier novel in its atmosphere. One early reviewer complained that *Popenjoy* "reminds us of a copper-plate by a good artist at its last stage.
All the finer touches, the tender, subtle gradations are worn out, and
strength is supplied by a hardening of the strongest lines. We are
among people who in a certain way recall . . . pleasant Barchester circles; but they are defined by very black lines indeed—all the delicacy
and nicety of touch is gone. The author used to be fond of his characters; but such lovingness finds no place here."[4]

The reviewer is reacting largely to the character of the repulsive
Marquis of Brotherton, elder brother of George Germain. The Marquis tyrannizes over his mother, sisters, and brother; and the question
of his child's legitimacy—whether the child of his questionable marriage to an Italian woman is legitimately Popenjoy—provides the basis of the novel's plot. *Is He Popenjoy?* differs from *Can You Forgive
Her?* because in the latter our sympathies are with Glencora and her
contemporaries; virtually all the focus is upon young people in their

twenties—with the comic Greenow plot creating ironic commentary through its use of older lovers. As long as Glencora can produce an heir, there will be no problems concerning who is heir or what place will be allotted to him. Moreover, the parents and substitute parents of *Can You Forgive Her?* are either absent, weak (like the indolent Mr. Vavasor), or relegated to the background as people who can annoy the younger generation by their advice (like Glencora's duennas). They are nuisances, for the most part, whose conservative views threaten to dampen the spirits of the younger generation. Both Trollope and his readers are situated to empathize with the young—not with the duennas.

In *Popenjoy* and many of the late novels, Trollope is still fascinated by the problems of marriage and social accommodation. But at the same time, he is no longer able to empathize so exclusively with the young, to overlook some of their foolishness, or to depict older relatives so stereotypically as the traditional conservative, blocking agents of comedy. Thus in *Is He Popenjoy?* we have the fascinating character of Dean Lovelace, the father of the heroine Mary. He has risen in life, with money derived from the stable and commerce, and aspires to have his daughter rise further. When he manages to marry his daughter to the younger brother of an apparently unmarried and childless marquis, he begins to hope that his grandson will be a marquis. This selfish motivation (along with a vulgar aggressiveness when his interests are concerned) makes him less attractive—or less comic—than the genial comic clergy of the Barchester novels, but we must not make the mistake of considering the dean unimportant or aberrant. The intensity of his concern for placing his daughter well in life is the same intensity, as we shall see, that dominates the duke's actions in *The Duke's Children* or Mr. Scarborough's in *Mr. Scarborough's Family*.

Dean Lovelace is vulnerable to criticism for having pushed Mary into a marriage without romance, for his rather vulgar insistence upon proving Popenjoy illegitimate, and for his advising Mary to enjoy herself in ways that irritate her husband and help cause a temporary estrangement between them. To the aristocratic (but stuffy) George Germain, his father-in-law's values often seem foreign or vulgar, and George is embarrassed at being a party to so obviously self-interested an enterprise as trying to prove Popenjoy illegitimate.

But while the reader is justified in disapproving of some of the dean's actions, the Germain family is also flawed by snobbery and weakness—its inability to protect the interests of all the members in the face of the tyrannical marquis. By the end when the suspect Italian Popenjoy and the marquis have both died and Mary's son has been born into the position of Popenjoy (the future Marquis), we are to believe that the older, more traditional values of the Germains are rightly and healthily balanced by the more self-assertive values of Dean Lovelace and that Mary can combine the best of both modes.

Despite the dean's vulgarity, Trollope has shown us that parents can feel intense concern for their children's position in the world and that activity may be necessary for safeguarding that position. Mary encounters the danger of being ignored, looked down upon, and constrained by the Germain ladies. She runs the risk of being neglected by George when he flirts with Adelaide Houghton. And she encounters the possibility of her child being deprived of his rightful place because of the domineering and corrupt marquis. In all these risks she needs a protector, and if we do not altogether approve of the style of the dean's protection, nevertheless we must admit that some protection is called for. In this way the late novels depart from the earlier ones in their recognition that life may not be as easy as it appears to the young and that the wisdom of their elders may be essential in preventing the very real dangers that can be encountered in a less than ideal society.

John Caldigate (1879)

Although superficially quite different in plot from *Is He Popenjoy?*, *John Caldigate* shares the intense concern with family and parent-child relations found in its predecessor. Just as Dean Lovelace's energetic determination to place his daughter well in life dominates the earlier novel and takes both admirable and less than admirable forms, so much of the determining energy of *John Caldigate* comes from parents' efforts to affect their children's lives. Initially this energy is seen in the father-son conflict between John Caldigate and his father, but their relationship is later upstaged by the mother-daughter conflict between Mrs. Bolton and her daughter. At issue are the entail, the validity of marriage, and inheritance—with the accusation of bigamy as the catalyzing agent for the family dynamics of this novel. *John Caldigate* is typical of the late Trollope novels in its fairly open treatment of Calidgate's living with a woman he did not marry and in the intensity of its focus upon the relation between generations.

The novel begins with strife between father and son; the first sentence reads, "Perhaps it was more the fault of Daniel Caldigate the father than of his son John Caldigate, that they two could not live together in comfort in the days of the young man's early youth" (1). Although discord between parent and child is not a new subject for Trollope in 1878, generational discord is treated in a new mode in *John Caldigate,* along with *The Duke's Children* and *Mr. Scarborough's Family.* Instead of the traditional comic mode, Trollope turns to a more probing psychological vein. John Hagan has written of *The Duke's Children* that the generational conflict is more subtle and poignant there than in the early novels, and the same may be said of *John Caldigate.*[5]

The initial estrangement between John and his father has several causes. The father's own introverted habits and silent, stern disposition have been reinforced by the death of his wife and daughters as well as by his distance from John, who was away at school. As with the duke in *The Duke's Children,* these habits of isolation impose barriers to communication and to the expression of the love each feels for the other. Moreover, Daniel Caldigate is jealous of his son's seeming difference from himself and is wounded by the boy's delight in hunting or sport with his maternal uncle, rather than in the more bookish concerns of his father: "He was jealous, jealous to hot anger, at being neglected, but could not bring himself to make advances to his own son" (1).

These misunderstandings grow to the point where the father essentially disinherits his son by paying him the value of the entail to free the entail. John needs the money to pay debts and is too proud to explain that he values the property he gives up when he accepts money in lieu of his inheritance.

The psychological distance between father and son and other barriers to their understanding each other are not overcome until after John's migration to Australia, the hardships he there encounters, and the mature manliness by which he succeeds at gold mining. He is then able to return to England with a surer sense of the value of the inheritance he has forfeited, but the father too has seen his own rashness. After John's return to England, they are both better able to express their feelings and so to understand one another. For instance, during John's first youthful indiscretion in acquiring debts, his father had distanced himself from the son in disapproval without expressing either the love he felt for his son or the grief he felt at disinheriting him. But a second, more trying circumstance in John's manhood leads his father to react differently. When John is falsely accused of bigamy, separated from his young wife and son, and imprisoned, Daniel Caldigate has the opportunity to act as he had done in the first trying circumstance—to separate himself, withdraw, or disapprove. Instead he strengthens his ties to John, becomes a father to his daughter-in-law, and in these ways fully commits himself to a family intimacy that had earlier been beyond his emotional range.

The second parent-child relation explored in the novel is that of Hester Bolton (who becomes John's wife) and her mother. The conflicts emanating from Mrs. Bolton are of a different nature than those seen in the relationship between John and his father. Mrs. Bolton provides perhaps Trollope's most interesting psychological study of a person in whom religious ideology exacerbates and interacts with psychological problems. In Mrs. Bolton, personal inhibition, desire for power, and maternal love all commingle with religious severity to create a tormented woman who drives, when she can, her daughter, her husband, and her stepsons. When John Caldigate proposes to marry Hester, Mrs. Bolton is horrified. She couches her objections in religious terms by objecting to his past indiscretions (his early debts, his having been a gold miner), but her real motivation is more complex. In part she does not want to share her daughter with anyone, to lose power over her daughter, or to allow her daughter a sexual life. Her allegations against Caldigate—before the marriage, early in the marriage when everything seems as it should be, and after the bigamy charge is brought forward—are always that he is an infidel, not a true believer, but the narrator reveals the underlying grounds of her fears and therefore her self-deception: "She suddenly perceived herself to be quite powerless with the child over whom her dominion had hitherto been supreme" (20).

When Caldigate is charged with bigamy, the Boltons contrive to lure Hester home and then to keep her prisoner there briefly. With a will as strong as her mother's, Hester refuses to go to bed after realizing that she is locked in the house, and spends the night sitting in the hall in defiance of her mother who grimly accompanies her there. Finally the male Boltons realize that Hester is too strong for them and that they will have to let her return to her husband, but Mrs. Bolton reacts in agony by saying, "I will not let you go. . . . I too can suffer. I too can endure. I will not be conquered by my own child" (36).

Hester's marriage is brought about despite Mrs. Bolton's opposition because Robert Bolton (a lawyer, child of old Mr. Bolton's first marriage) and his brothers convince their father that Mrs. Bolton should not be allowed to keep Hester a virtual prisoner isolated from all human contact. More worldly and pragmatic than Mrs. Bolton, they consider Caldigate a prosperous choice for Hester to marry. Even had it not been for her initial fears about Caldigate's morals, Mrs. Bolton would probably have objected to the marriage because it occasions a power struggle in which she proves to be less powerful than her stepsons to direct her husband's decisions. As the narrator explains, "There was no touch of hypocrisy about her. . . . She did not know that the convictions on which she rested with such confidence had come in truth from her injured pride,—had settled themselves in her mind because she had been beaten in her endeavours to prevent her daughter's marriage" (22). So she continues to disapprove of the wedding, and when Caldigate is accused of bigamy she seizes the opportunity to try to assert herself again over her husband and stepsons.

Her husband and stepsons act in the pragmatic way one might expect of the male relatives of a woman whose husband is accused of bigamy. They want to protect her from him, have her return home to their family, and have Caldigate punished. But when the pardon is granted and there is every reason to believe Caldigate has not committed bigamy, the Bolton males realize—even though some of them are still quite resentful of Caldigate—that they must recognize the marriage out of fairness and a desire to support Hester. The male Boltons' reactions may be seen as further variations upon Trollope's fascination in the late novels with parents' desires to protect their children. Their reactions are strong, sometimes offensive to Hester, Caldigate, and the reader, but certainly within the normal range of behavior for Trollope's parents. What is fascinating about Mrs. Bolton's response is that she goes so far beyond the normal fears or protectiveness—even to the point of potentially endangering Hester's happiness and security in marriage. She is rather like Louis Trevelyan of *He Knew He Was Right* in having an extreme version of psychological traits present in lesser degree in the rest of the novel's characters.

The psychological exploration of parent-child relations in *John Caldigate* is well matched to the plot's emphasis upon inheritance, the entail, marriage, and bigamy. Throughout history, marriage, when legal, has been one of society's primary devices for preserving property and passing it on to the next generation. So the question of whether

John Caldigate will be his father's heir is extremely important both in economic terms and in terms of the continuation of the family— as is the question later of whether John's son will be John's heir (this depends on whether he is the legitimate offspring of a legal marriage). Hester's place in life will also be determined by the legality of her marriage. Not only does *John Caldigate* demonstrate the aging Trollope's concern for the parental perspective, but there has been a shift from the earlier novels' emphasis upon self-realization. In *Can You Forgive Her?* the major characters are all involved in a process of self-discovery and self-realization—the successful translation of identity into a position in the world and the successful negotiation of one's needs in a marriage. In *Is He Popenjoy?* the self-realization theme is still strong, but it is accompanied by a different perspective—the dean's desire to make his daughter's position secure above and beyond her own desires in her marriage. In *John Caldigate* the dimension of self-realization is further relegated to the background, replaced by the more conservative perspective of age. At issue is not simply John's or Hester's happiness in marriage, for we know relatively little about them as individuals compared to what we knew of Glencora or Alice Vavasor in *Can You Forgive Her?*. Instead what is paramount is the safety, legality, and prosperity of the process by which parent secures a place for the child and that child eventually secures a place for the next generation.

The Duke's Children (1880)

Most readers would judge *The Duke's Children* to be the finest of Trollope's late novels, perhaps even the finest of all his works. John Hagan, writing of the "wealth of tenderness and subtlety" in *The Duke's Children* says that "on the strength of this novel alone one is tempted to claim [Trollope] as one of the most unostentatious yet sensitive psychological novelists in the whole range of nineteenth-century English fiction."[6] Yet *The Duke's Children* is not an isolated achievement. The duke's intense concern for his children's marriages resembles Dean Lovelace's intense desire in *Is He Popenjoy?* to see his daughter and her children well situated or Mrs. Bolton's desire in *John Caldigate* to determine how and whether her daughter marries— even though the forms their concerns take differ greatly.

These novels, along with *Mr. Scarborough's Family* are interrelated by three issues: (1) the strength of the parent's interest in enhancing his or her child's place in life, (2) the question of which generation has power, along with the strong sense in these late novels that power is passing from the older generation to the younger, and (3) the sometimes painful recognition on the parents' parts that their children are individuals in their own right and that at some point the parent will lack power because the child will act for him- or herself.

Each of these three concerns is readily apparent in *The Duke's Children*. First, the duke, who had hitherto concerned himself with politics and allowed Glencora to manage the children, finds after Glencora's death (at the novel's beginning) how distressing it is to try to direct his children into the paths he approves of and how strong are his children's tendencies to go in directions he does not approve. Lady Mary's desire to marry Frank Tregear is distressing because Tregear, though a gentleman, is not of their class and has no income of his own. The duke fears Tregear is an adventurer, concerned only to gain Mary's money.

Aside from Mary's obstinacy about Tregear and the distress the duke feels at seeing her grief, Mary herself is all that she should be in his eyes, but the duke's two sons are not. Silverbridge, his eldest son and heir, gets into one scrape after another; he is expelled from college, is partially responsible for his younger brother's being expelled, associates with a horse enthusiast, Captain Tifto, who is beneath him in class and ultimately is responsible for Silverbridge's losing eighty thousand pounds in betting upon their jointly owned horse.

Though he comes from a higher social class, Silverbridge is like Johnny Eames in being a hobbledehoy—a young man who has great promise but matures slowly and makes many errors during his initiation into society. As might be expected from the other late novels, however, the late-maturing young man is here viewed from a different vantage point than in the case of Johnny Eames. The young man is not seen as a surrogate for reader or author; instead, the reader views Silverbridge through the perspective of Silverbridge's father, the duke—and at times through that of Lady Mabel Grex who, because she feels so much older and more jaded than Silverbridge, looks tolerantly down upon his youthful awkwardness and his growing maturity.

The duke's distress and sense of helplessness are made poignant in the following passage:

Though the father and the two young men were living together they did not see very much of each other. The Duke breakfasted at nine and the repast was a very simple one. When they failed to appear, he did not scold,—but would simply be disappointed. At dinner they never met. . . . It was not often that he reproached them or preached to them. Though he could not live with them on almost equal terms, as some fathers can live with their sons, though he could not laugh at their fun or make them laugh at his wit, he knew that it would have been better both for him and them if he had possessed this capacity. (25)

And yet the more Silverbridge errs and senses his father's disappointment, the more he feels for his father's distress until finally the two are brought closer together emotionally and in their views of life.

After Gerald is expelled from Cambridge (through Silverbridge's irresponsibility, in part), Silverbridge attempts to comfort his father, telling him that he had studied and passed along to Gerald the letter of advice the Duke had sent Silverbridge. The narrator then comments, "There was something sweet and pleasant in the young man's manner by which the father could hardly not be captivated" (25). The relation between the duke and Silverbridge somewhat resembles that between Daniel and John Caldigate as they move from distance toward closeness, and it is the opposite of the relation depicted in *Mr. Scarborough's Family* where the father grows more and more cynical about his sons. If one message of the late novels is the powerlessness of the parent to influence his children (particularly in *Mr. Scarborough's Family* but in *The Duke's Children* also), nevertheless there is a strong sense in *The Duke's Children* of the compensating sweetness and emotional fulfillment a parent feels about his children even though they frustrate and disappoint him.[7]

One of the most poignant scenes in *The Duke's Children* comes after the duke has told Silverbridge that he would give up much of his property and income to Silverbridge if the latter married; when Silverbridge replies "I can't bear to hear you talking of giving up anything" (26), the duke is moved: "Then the father looked round the room furtively, and seeing that the door was shut, and that they were assuredly alone, he put out his hand and gently stroked the young man's hair. It was almost a caress,—as though he would have said to himself, 'Were he my daughter, I would kiss him' " (26).

James Kincaid writes of Silverbridge's relation to his father, "As he mellows and matures he moves closer to the position held by the Duke. . . . Silverbridge has all along been protected from extremes by his fine gentlemanly instincts, especially by his natural modesty, his capacity for self-doubt. . . . He amazes his father by the sensitiv-

ity he displays in understanding that Sir Timothy is using him only
to annoy the Duke. . . . His vision and stability in this case have sur-
passed his father's. He has demonstrated an open and unembarrassed
love, responding in this political reversal with a simple integration of
private affection and public action that astounds his father."[8] Despite
his own initial awkwardness with them, the strength of the duke's
love and concern for his children, together with the model he represents, has in effect produced a son who is worthy of his father—who,
despite temperamental and generational differences, ultimately matures into a son his father can be proud of.

Perhaps the difference in the portrait of the two hobbledehoys—
John Eames and Silverbridge—is that Eames is a surrogate for Trollope as a young man, and so the reader views Eames with the sympathy derived from imagining him- or herself in Eames's situation,
entering upon maturity with all the frustration of not quite being
mature yet. But in *The Duke's Children,* it is the duke, not Silverbridge, who is the surrogate for Trollope. The reader sees from the
perspective of the parent or some other older person looking back be-
nignly at the struggles of youth, full of hope that the younger generation, despite its flaws, will eventually prove itself to be emotionally
joined to the older generation and willing to respect the lessons of the
past. Critics have generally acknowledged *The Duke's Children* to be
both a conservative novel (in its emphasis on preserving what the
duke has achieved) and a hopeful novel (in that the young, despite
their rebellion, eventually reaffirm most of the duke's values). Its perspective upon the younger generation accounts for both the conservatism and the hope.

Nevertheless, in the midst of this optimism is the theme of power
and its passing from one generation to the next. The duke's children
have the power to thwart their father or to make their own choices,
but his own power, the duke discovers, is sadly diminished. In trying
to choose a husband for his daughter and a wife for Silverbridge, he
fails altogether. He is able, theoretically, to refuse assent to the marriages they choose or to withhold money, but his ability to do either
proves illusory; he loves his children too much to see them unhappy,
and so when they prove determined enough to assert their own
choices, he cannot bear to refuse assent. Thus while his love for them
is strong enough to make them want to please him, it also strips from
him the ability to refuse them what they want.

The Duke's Children thus concludes the Palliser series by chronicling

how the man who has been one of the wealthiest and most eminent
men in all England, who has been prime minister, finds power slip-
ping from him as his children mature. The series has in a sense paralleled the course of Trollope's own adult life; it begins with the stories
of self-realization in marriage and politics in *Can You Forgive Her?*,
proceeds to the story of Phineas Finn's self-realization and then disillusion, and finally moves to the disappointments of middle and old
age. In this final novel, the duke at times grieves over his loss of
power: "There is nothing so wretched to a man as yielding. Young
people and women have to yield,—but for such a man as this, to
yield is in itself a misery" (50). When Silverbridge insists on marrying the American Isabel Boncassen, the duke exclaims in frustration,
"My opinion is to go for nothing,—in anything!" (71). Or when
forced to yield about Tregear, he exclaims, "Do you think that a man
can be thwarted in everything and not feel it?" (74).

Still this relinquishing of power is accompanied by its own com-
pensation:

> It was sweet to him to have something to caress. Now in the solitude of his
> life, as years were coming on him, he felt how necessary it was that he should
> have someone who would love him. Since his wife had left him he had been
> debarred from these caresses by the necessity of showing his antagonism to
> her dearest wishes. It has been his duty to be stern. . . . He was not pre-
> pared to acknowledge that [the duty of separating Mary from Tregear] had
> ceased;—but yet there had crept over him a feeling that as he was half con-
> quered, why should he not seek some recompense in his daughter's love? (66)

The duke seems thus to represent Trollope's view of the sorrow and
sweetness of age; it is not comforting for men like Daniel Caldigate,
the duke, or Mr. Scarborough to see power pass from their hands or
to see their children go their own way heedless of their father's
wishes, but the luckier fathers, Caldigate and the duke, find new joys
to solace them, in part, for their losses.

Finally, then, the parent must recognize that the child is an individual in his or her own right and that the parent's ability to decide
for the child must diminish. The psychological subtlety of *The Duke's
Children* derives, as John Hagan has argued, from Trollope's depiction
of the duke's struggles with his own scarcely conscious need to relive
and justify his marriage to Glencora.[9] The duke sees in Lady Mary's
love for Tregear a parallel to Glencora's earlier love for Burgo Fitzgerald. A victim of self-doubt, the duke still remembers how Glencora

loved Burgo but was forced by relatives to reject Burgo and enter into a more rational marriage. So at first he finds Mary's determination to marry Tregear personally threatening, though he manages to rationalize his fears in other ways. He fears that Mary's preference shows Glencora should have married Fitzgerald and that Glencora's encouragement of Tregear shows that she never overcame her preference for Fitzgerald. So the duke, in trying to prevent Tregear from marrying Mary, is trying to justify the wisdom of his marriage to Glencora— both its value to him and its value to her in preventing her ruin at Fitzgerald's hands.

But Mary is not Glencora, nor Tregear Fitzgerald. Mary has a steadiness gained more from her father than her mother, and Tregear is a far safer marital prospect than Fitzgerald was. From the reader's perspective, the marriage of Mary and Tregear may even be seen as a successful union of the best qualities in Glencora and the duke, one devoid of the friction between the exuberantly irresponsible Glencora and the overly prosaic duke.

Although at first the duke sees only the threat to his self-justification, eventually he learns to free himself from the past and to see Mary and Tregear as themselves, rather than as projections of Glencora and his youthful self. In sanctioning the marriage of Mary to Tregear, it may be argued, the duke frees himself, triumphs over some of his past failures, and thereby offers grounds for believing that the relation between generations may lead to harmony and growth.

Ayala's Angel (1881)

Like the other late Trollope novels, *Ayala's Angel* provides interpretive difficulties for readers. Some critics have described it as a light-hearted romance or a comedy, even if they have felt the need therefore to dissociate it from the rest of Trollope's late novels.[10] Other critics find in it an undercutting of romantic views.[11] One way of confronting this interpretive problem is to consider how *Ayala's Angel* fits, yet still departs from traditional comedy and how, in doing so, it aligns itself with the less cheerful late novels here discussed.

Northrop Frye describes the basic formula of comedy (from Greek drama to the modern novel): "What normally happens is that a young man wants a young woman, that his desire is resisted by some opposition, usually paternal, and that near the end of the play some twist in the plot enables the hero to have his will. . . . At the beginning

of the play the obstructing characters are in charge of the play's
society. . . . At the end of the play the device in the plot that brings
hero and heroine together causes a new society to crystallize around
the hero."[12] The new society is usually signaled by a ritual—most often by weddings.

If we apply this formula to *The Duke's Children*, its relevance is immediately apparent. The duke initially possesses power and provides
obstacles to his children's desires, but eventually their wishes prove
too strong for him, and at the end of the novel the duke has acknowledged his limits and agreed to their marriages, thereby implicitly acknowledging the loosening of class barriers. What separates *The
Duke's Children* as comedy from earlier comedies like *Barchester Towers,
Can You Forgive Her?,* or *Rachel Ray* is, however, as we have seen,
that the reader has a great deal of sympathy with the duke's opposition and is somewhat distanced from the young heroes and heroines.

Seen in this light, *Ayala's Angel* recognizably resembles *The Duke's
Children* more than the earlier comedies. In a conventional comedy
like *Rachel Ray,* the parental figures (Mrs. Ray, Mrs. Prime, Mr.
Comfort, and Mr. Tappitt) all create obstacles to the courtship of Rachel and Luke and are seen to some degree as foolish. Luke's triumph
over Mr. Tappitt at the end represents the triumph of youth over age,
and the reader may feel little sympathy for the comic Tappitt's forced
retirement. In *The Duke's Children* and *Ayala's Angel,* however, the
comic formula is preserved, but the attitude toward old versus young
is reversed. The old are seen as wise or well-intentioned while the
young are often rude, foolish, or self-deceived. Nevertheless, the
young, by the energy and power of their youth, manage to blunder
ahead with their plans while their well-meaning elders do the best
they can to minimize the effects of the youthful mistakes.

In *Ayala's Angel* there are four parental figures suddenly forced into
new responsibilities by the death of the parents of the heroines, Ayala
and Lucy Dormer. Reginald Dosett and his wife are a childless couple, genteel but only by great care able to avoid poverty. When Lucy
Dormer is assigned to them for care (Reginald being her maternal uncle), the lack of sympathy between Aunt Dosett and the responsible
but hitherto spoiled Lucy is shown with a comedy more grim than
lighthearted. Mrs. Dosett is severe and is distressed to know that her
regular household economies must be increased to accommodate a
niece who will not understand or enter with sympathy into the need
for such thrift. Trollope allows Mrs. Dosett to appear fairly sympa-

thetic despite her personal unattractiveness and her inability to deal with her niece. Mr. Dosett is similarly ineffectual; though the reader may find the generational disharmony comic and the Dosetts unattractive, nevertheless their good intentions and the sacrifices they make almost mutely for their unappreciative nieces cause them to evoke less stereotypical reactions than the comic parents and duennas of Trollope's early comedies.

The girls' other aunt, Lady Tringle, is better situated in life but no better able to deal with her nieces. She initially chooses the more striking Ayala as her ward, only to find that Ayala is rude to her cousin Augusta and that cousin Tom Tringle has fallen in love with her: "Ayala had turned out on her hands something altogether different from the girl she had intended to cherish and patronise. Ayala was independent; superior rather than inferior to her own girls; more thought of by others; apparently without any touch of that subservience which should have been produced in her by her position. Ayala seemed to demand as much as though she were a daughter of the house, and at the same time to carry herself as though she were more gifted than the daughters of the house. She was less obedient even than a daughter" (8). Lady Tringle would be distressed to have her son marry Ayala, but she is even more upset to hear Ayala call Tom a "stupid lout" (8) and reject him as beneath her.

Ayala's rudeness to all the female Tringles, Tom's despair, and Ayala's anger at him finally lead the Tringles to propose a switch with the Dosetts, so out of similar frustrations the Dosetts give up Lucy for Ayala and the Tringles give up Ayala for Lucy. Both sets of guardians hope to acquire a more docile and sympathetic niece through the exchange, and both girls remain fairly obtuse to the suffering they have inflicted on their guardians through tactless or selfish behavior.

The most important of the four guardians is Sir Thomas Tringle. Though he is not related by blood to either of the girls, he has money, power, good will, and a rather appealing, blunt common sense. Sir Thomas becomes responsible, then, for five young people of courtship age—his three children (Augusta, Tom, and Gertrude) and his two nieces. The four girls alone require him to deal with six male suitors, and most of the ten young people are comically foolish or hard to deal with. The comedy, though, is determined less by the traditional obstacles that the old impose on the young than by the difficulties the young inflict on the old.

For instance, Sir Thomas's eldest daughter, Augusta, marries a

sponger who, after being endowed with one hundred twenty thousand
pounds from Sir Thomas, continues to live at Sir Thomas's houses,
altogether insensitive to the latter's increasingly pointed jibes about
his presence. His second daughter, Gertrude, is attracted to a fortune
hunter, Frank Houston, who does not love Gertrude but needs to
marry for money. Gertrude proves very stubborn but is finally overwhelmed by the combination of Sir Thomas's refusal to give money to
Houston and Houston's subsequent withdrawal. Though vanquished,
however, Gertrude persists in being foolish. She next tries unsuccessfully to elope to Ostend with Captain Batsby, thereby eliciting comments from Sir Thomas like "Why is it that my children are so much
more foolish than other people's?" (48).

His son Tom acts the fool by falling in love with Ayala and then
finding himself unable to overcome his feeling for her despite her indifference (even contempt). He moons about, drinks, and gets into a
fight with Captain Stubbs (the man Ayala eventually marries), making of himself a ridiculous and pathetic figure until Sir Thomas sends
him off to America to recover. Yet the narrator's attitude toward the
rejected Tom is not as simple as the narrator's attitude toward the
rejected Slope in *Barchester Towers*. He says of Tom:

A very vulgar and foolish young man! But a young man capable of a persis-
tent passion! Young men not foolish and not vulgar are, perhaps common
enough. But the young men of constant heart and capable of such persistency
as Tom's are not to be found every day walking about the streets of the
metropolis. . . . Tom Tringle had everything against him,—everything that
would weigh with Ayala; and yet he fought his battle out to the last gasp.
Therefore, I desire my hearers to regard Tom Tringle as the hero of the transactions with which they have been concerned, and to throw their old shoes
after him as he starts away upon his grand tour. (61)

This complex attitude—seeing what is ridiculous in Tom while maintaining some distance from Ayala by finding her also at fault—is perhaps more prevalent in Trollope's later novels than his early ones.

Sir Thomas's troubles with Ayala's and Lucy's courtships are that
Ayala persistently refuses three suitors (Stubbs among them) before
discovering her love for Stubbs. Lucy does the opposite, falling in
love with a young artist without means and then stubbornly refusing
to change her mind, despite Sir Thomas's conviction that Hamel's artistic principles are going to prevent him from being able to support
a wife.

In all these troubles, Sir Thomas's sharp tongue is made enjoyable to the reader while the young people's activities are viewed from a perspective rather like Sir Thomas's—the perspective of genial cynicism. At the end, for instance, the reader is presented with the sort of comic dialogue Jane Austen used in *Northanger Abbey* to reveal the comic egocentrism of Mrs. Allen and Mrs. Thorpe through their conversational hobbyhorses:

> To Lucy, Isadore Hamel was, at the present moment, the one hero walking the face of this sublunary globe; and to Ayala, as we all know, Jonathan Stubbs was an Angel of Light, and, therefore, more even than a hero. As each spoke, the "He's" intended took a different personification; so that to any one less interested than the young ladies themselves there might be some confusion as to which "He" might at that moment be under discussion. "It was bad," said Lucy, "when Uncle Tom told him to sell those magnificent conceptions of his brain by auction!"
> "I did feel for him certainly," said Ayala.
> "And then when he was constrained to say that he would take me at once without any preparation because Aunt Emmeline wanted me to go, I don't suppose any man ever behaved more beautifully than he did." (63)

And so they continue, each absorbed in her own concerns and ignoring the other's. This gentle mockery of his heroines is a symptom of Trollope's distance from them.

Several critics have analyzed seriously the process of Ayala's relinquishing (or fulfilling) her dream image in marrying Stubbs, but such an interpretation makes of *Ayala's Angel* a novel of self-realization rather like *Can You Forgive Her?* or *Phineas Finn*.[13] Instead the theme of Ayala's selfhood should be seen as subordinate to the comedy of the guardians' frustrated attempts to direct the young; in this way *Ayala's Angel* reveals its kinship to a novel written only three years later, *Mr. Scarborough's Family*. The young people of the comic *Ayala's Angel* survive or triumph despite their follies while in *Mr. Scarborough's Family* both Mountjoy and Augustus Scarborough are undone by their follies, but nevertheless in both novels the central actor of the comedy is an aging man who tries to protect and provide for the young while having to lament their foolishness.

Mr. Scarborough's Family (1883)

Interpretations of *Mr. Scarborough's Family* are at least as divergent as those of any other Trollope novel with readers' reactions to Mr.

Scarborough's maneuvers on behalf of his sons ranging from admiration to condemnation.[14] But whatever one's ethical judgment upon Mr. Scarborough, this novel's kinship to the other late Trollope novels needs to be made clear. Once again—like *Popenjoy* or *John Caldigate*—the plot turns upon the question of the legitimacy of possible heirs; once again the focus is upon the dynamics of the family, rather than upon society as a whole; and once again the pivot of decision making is an old man. Like the Dean of Brotherton, Daniel Caldigate and Mrs. Bolton, the Duke of Omnium, and Sir Thomas Tringle, Mr. Scarborough is determined to advance the interests of his heirs but frustrated in the attempt. Like the other novels, this one demonstrates the folly of the young, though with a good deal less optimism, and like the other old men, Mr. Scarborough learns the limits of his power.

Trollope, who was unknowingly close to death when he wrote *Mr. Scarborough's Family* in 1881, seems to have created almost a fantasy plot for a man of his age wishing to exert the utmost of his power to determine what his sons should do; in the struggle between generations, Mr. Scarborough aspires to a victory in which even on the brink of the grave the father can outwit his sons, his lawyers, and his sons' creditors. By manipulating the evidence about his marriage, Mr. Scarborough is first able to convince the world that his spendthrift eldest son, Mountjoy, is illegitimate. By doing so he bankrupts Mountjoy but thereby preserves the family wealth from Mountjoy's vulturelike creditors who are ready to swallow the estate on Scarborough's death. Then when the younger son, Augustus, comes to terms with the creditors (out of his own self-interest in preventing legal squabbles), Mr. Scarborough is able to outwit the world—and his younger son—a second time by proving the elder son to be legitimate after all. This restores the inheritance, now freed from debt, to the elder son.

This rather Machiavellian maneuvering by Mr. Scarborough has elicited admiration from some readers; and, with Trollope's characteristic double vision, he may even have viewed Scarborough's manipulations as an enjoyable fantasy at a time when he was close to death and somewhat disappointed in both his sons. Nevertheless, Trollope does not allow the fantasy free play; subtly through the rest of the novel he comments upon and judges Mr. Scarborough. The sympathy readers have felt for Mr. Scarborough derives not so much from their approval of him as from the sympathy that we might feel for anyone who in old age, on the verge of dying, discovers that he has failed at what has been most important to him. His actions, however, are not condoned. As Roger Slakey has argued, Mr. Scarborough has failed to understand human relationships, been insensitive to his sons' feelings, played favorites, taught his sons to hate each other and mistrust him, and failed to teach them loyalty, love, or respect.[15] His system has defeated the very ends he sought because ultimately neither son has been worthy of the money, and Mountjoy, who eventually inherits it all, is incapable of holding onto it.

The judgment upon or condemnation of Mr. Scarborough comes, then, from the outcome of the main plot, but the two minor plots, in a characteristically Trollopian manner, function to maintain the complexity of the situation and sympathy for the characters. In one minor plot, Mr. Prosper is a foolish old man (the opposite of Scarborough, in this regard) who considers disinheriting his heir Harry Annesley, because the latter has failed to show affection and respect for Mr. Prosper. Despite Prosper's comic foolishness and our sympathy for Harry, we are shown that Harry has indeed failed to give his uncle the affection he needs. Thus Harry becomes another example in Trollope's late novels of the young who take and do not give. In conjunction with the major plot, this minor plot functions to increase our sympathy for old men while still showing the silliness—or harmfulness—of their attempts to preserve power from passing naturally to their heirs.

A second minor plot is less comic. Mr. Grey, who has acted honorably as Mr. Scarborough's lawyer, experiences personal sorrows of two sorts that illuminate the novel's themes. Within his own family, Mr. Grey is more lucky than Scarborough in that his own goodness and upright conduct have resulted in a daughter worthy of him, a daughter who is a great comfort to him. But he is also powerless to influence the young in several ways; he is unable to convince his daughter to marry because of her almost incestuous attachment to him, and he is equally unable to help settle his nieces happily and honorably in life. His second source of sorrow is that Mr. Scarborough's dishonesty compromises Mr. Grey. Though Grey has acted honestly on Scarborough's behalf in helping him to disinherit first Mountjoy and then Augustus, when Scarborough's dishonesty becomes known, it appears as if Mr. Grey has knowingly cooperated in his attempt to defraud the creditors. Thus Grey is compromised and feels he must withdraw from the law; since the law has been almost his whole life, this forced retirement constitutes a personal tragedy for him. If there were no other means of judging Mr. Scarborough to be immoral, the impact of Scarborough's actions on Grey alone would suffice to pass judgment on his immorality.

Mr. Scarborough's Family and the other late novels deserve more recognition than they have received for their innovations in the history of the novel. Novels have traditionally dealt with the young, depicting their struggles to achieve a place in society and a sense of self. Trollope's late novels testify, however, that there are dramas and struggles inherent in other stages in life and that those dramas can be turned into engaging and thought-provoking fiction.

Chapter Eight
Conclusion: Trollope's Reputation

Trollope's reputation has been affected by a number of variables: by changing literary tastes, by the immensity of his literary output, by the deceptively simple nature of his novels, and by his own willingness at times to misrepresent himself. Bradford Booth wrote in 1958 that there was "nothing in literary history to match the divided opinion on Trollope's novels."[1] During Trollope's lifetime and in the century since his death, the discussion about his achievements has shifted, but the general nature of the discussion has remained fairly constant. For simplicity, we may divide the discussion of his reputation into three periods: contemporary Victorian reaction during Trollope's lifetime, the reaction against mid-Victorianism in the late nineteenth-century and its continuing influence, and the modern reassessment of Trollope's achievement.

Trollope's Reputation among His Contemporaries

Among Trollope's contemporaries, three perceptions were particularly important. First, as we may see in the following passage from Richard Holt Hutton (written at the time of Trollope's death), Trollope's subjects were seen as morally wholesome and wide ranging: "—the ardent admiration with which he always painted humility and unworldliness . . . and the sense of something like moral wonder with which he regarded them;—the profound respect which he entertained for public spirit like that of his second 'Duke of Omnium,' and the charity with which he regarded the authority of family traditions . . . —the scorn which he felt for all the knavery of commercial Rings."[2] Hutton goes on to praise Trollope's explorations of commerce, politics, honor, and love for their strength and rightness of feeling, as well as, by implication, for their accuracy.

A second perception and ground for praise, then, was that Trollope was gifted in his realism, in what his contemporaries saw as the accu-

racy of his portraits. Nathaniel Hawthorne was not alone in his sense
that Trollope's novels were "just as real as if some giant had hewn a
great lump out of the earth."[3] Sometimes Trollope's depictions were
described as photographic. But, however it was stated, the praise for
Trollope's verisimilitude was often accompanied by disparagements of
his imagination or intellect. For instance, a reviewer wrote in 1861,
"In all his works . . . there is not a touch of original fancy; as far as
it is possible for a novelist to be without invention he is without it.
There is no ingenuity in the construction of his stories. The sketches
of character on which they depend for their value are the result of
shrewd observation cleverly expressed in every-day phrase; never of
any subtle or peculiar insight into character."[4]

   The notion that no imagination or insight is required for depicting
realistic characters should seem blatantly false to us by now, but the
idea was forceful in Trollope's day and continues to some extent in
ours. So it is useful to look further at such claims. A *Saturday Review*
critic (already influenced by that journal's hosility toward popular
taste and serial publication) wrote of *Framley Parsonage:*

All [Trollope's characters] are ordinary men and women, and their sayings
and doings are neither above nor below the level of what we see in common
and everyday life. Mr. Trollope himself nowhere pretends to do more than
to write down what he sees going on around him. He paints from the
outside. . . . In fact, he is far less of a novelist than a good diner-out. Any
of Mr. Trollope's admirers who has a strong sense of fun may do for himself
in imagination what it is Mr. Trollope's charm that he has done so well on
paper. Given Mrs. Proudie and Mrs. Grantley in a room, who does not know
what they would say to one another? The difference between Mr. Trollope
and his readers is that he not only knows what Mrs. Proudie and Mrs. Grantley would say, and how they would look, but can seize upon the most amus-
ing points and write them down.[5]

The reviewer, then, assumes that all of us, as diners-out, have the
raw material for a *Barchester Towers* within us, but that most of us
simply do not write down our novels. It should seem to be a prepos-
terous idea—easily refuted by the fact that we have not all become
famous, best-selling novelists. But such statements can still be heard
today about popular fiction of our time, so we need to realize that
fiction that is realistic and has popular appeal is most likely to receive
this kind of disparagement.

   Combined with the perception that Trollope was wholesome and realistic, then, was a third perception—that something lacking in Trollope prevented him from rising into the first rank of novelists. Such a notion is clear in Hutton, who after extolling Trollope's handling of an extraordinary range of subjects (passion, sexual relations, ethical conduct, family relations, social relations, public spirit, political conduct, and economic problems), then continues by saying, "On the other hand, it is clear that there was little or no disposition in Mr. Trollope to pierce much deeper than the social surface of life. It is not often that he takes us into the world of solitary feeling at all, and of the power of the positive influence of their religion over men.[6]

The sense that there was something missing in Trollope was widespread; upon Trollope's death the *Times* critic predicted that he would not rank with the great novelists of the century—Scott, Balzac, Dickens, George Sand, George Eliot, Charlotte Brontë, Thackeray, or Turgenev—but among the second rank with Austen and Gaskell who wrote "realistic studies of English domestic life."[7] There are at least three assumptions implied in this kind of assessment: (1) realism is easy to write because it merely copies nature and therefore involves little genius or inspiration on the part of the writer; (2) domestic life is less interesting or important than the larger arena of society and politics; and (3) the surfaces of life show only something "superficial" about life. Among Trollope's contemporaries, these preudices were never entirely erased—even for his admirers. Each of these assumptions has been challenged to some degree in our age, but each has remained difficult to remove from people's perceptions.

The Aesthetic Influence

At the end of the nieteenth century, a new emphasis upon art for its own sake helped to make Trollope appear old-fashioned. A number of factors were involved—the lingering influence of romanticism, the widening gap between popular taste and the tastes of an intellectual or artistic coterie, and a reaction against the mid-Victorian moral emphasis (viewed as overly stuffy by a younger generation). The more blatant rebellions against Victorian seriousness by a man like Oscar Wilde were important at the time, but through the first part of the twentieth century what was more important was the emergence of a new approach to novel writing. Writers like Flaubert, Henry James, James Joyce, Joseph Conrad, Virginia Woolf, or William Faulkner became the norm both for those trying to write novels and those theo-

rizing about them. Their novels were more compact than the sprawl-
ing, multi-plot novels of Trollope, Dickens, George Eliot, or
Thackeray had been. The modern novels were read by a more elite
audience (scorn for popular tastes having intensified) and emphasized
greater attention to language, strategies to avoid an overt narrative
persona, and a less bourgeois milieu.[8]

The generation following Trollope, therefore, disparaged his novels
largely because of its own rejection of parts of the realist tradition and
its notion of the role of the artist. This rejection then played a role
in Trollope's reputation for much of the twentieth century. Henry
James's comments (1883) are especially illuminating. After assigning
Trollope to a level below Dickens, Thackeray, and George Eliot,
James criticizes four features of Trollope's novels in particular. First,
Trollope published too much, showed a "prodigious" fecundity, a
"gross, importunate" fertility, while writing in a mechanical way.[9]
Second, his language was heavy-footed with "no more pretensions to
style than if it were cut out of yesterday's newspaper" (p. 532).
Third, Trollope failed to take himself seriously as an artist (pp. 526–
27); he made, in James's eyes, the appalling error of admitting that
he was constructing an artifice when his narrator intruded upon
the story and admitted it was only a story (pp. 535–36). Similarly,
Trollope "never played with a subject, never juggled with the sympathies or the credulity of his reader, was never in the least paradoxical
or mystifying (p. 529), a criticism that amounts, in part, to com-
plaining that Trollope was not Henry James. Finally, James implies
criticism in the very terms of his praise. He commends Trollope's
"complete appreciation of the usual" in terms that reveal how unself-
conscious James assumes Trollope to have been:

[W]ith his eyes comfortably fixed on the familiar, the actual . . . his great
distinction is that in resting there his vision took in so much of the field.
And then he *felt* all daily and immediate things as well as saw them; felt
them in a simple, direct, salubrious way, with their sadness, their gladness,
their charm, their comicality, all their obvious and measurable
meanings. . . . [He] was content to go on indefinitely watching the life that
surrounded him, and holding up his mirror to it. . . . The striking thing to
the critic was that his robust and patient mind had no particular bias, his
imagination no light of its own. . . . If he was in any degree a man of genius
(and I hold that he was), it was in virtue of this happy, instinctive perception
of human varieties. His knowledge of the stuff we are made of, his observation of the common behaviour of men and women, was not reasoned nor
acquired, not even particularly studied. (pp. 527–29)

To James, who clearly valued self-conscious artistry, Trollope appeared a simple, perhaps naive writer, who did not consciously know what he was doing and who served as a sort of conduit for mirroring the life outside him without either distortion or deep understanding. It apparently did not occur to James to question this assumption—to wonder how such perceptive portrayals could be created without effort or self-consciousness.

James's perceptions and assumptions have been echoed over and over since Trollope's day; their context, therefore, deserves further scrutiny. The first of his assumptions, that Trollope published too much, is in one sense certainly true. Critics and readers in his day could not always keep up with his tremendous output, and even when they could there was a natural human tendency to devalue what they already had in abundance. But beyond this reaction lay a more questionable assumption—that a true artist could not write so prolifically, that only a more mechanical talent could write so much. This idea had been fed by romanticism and then gained strength in the late nineteenth century with writers like James who turned away from trying to write novels with broad popular appeal.

The belief that romantic inspiration and careful artistry were superior to mechanical, workmanlike literary production was a prejudice that Trollope, who was far from naive about writing, understood perfectly well—and then purposely flouted. By the time that he wrote the *Autobiography* in 1875–76, he had sensed enough of the literary prejudices of his day to begin experimenting in his own novels and to know that others would belittle him for his writing habits, yet he made no attempt to accommodate that prejudice.

Instead he emphasized the speed and regularity of his working habits—perhaps even exaggerated them in order to shock and annoy people like James.[10] He kept a diary to record how many pages he wrote each week; the average was 40 pages, but it ranged from 20 on a bad week to 112 on a good one. He counted each word and prided himself on always delivering to the publisher almost exactly the number of words he had proposed to write (*Autobiography*, pp. 100–101). He had himself awakened regularly every morning so that he would be at his desk by 5:30, ready to work there for three hours, using his watch to make sure that he wrote 250 words every quarter hour (*Autobiography*, p. 227). If this regularity and productivity were not already enough to shock critics, Trollope further caused them to deprecate him by commenting, "I have been told that such appliances [his work habits] are beneath the notice of a man of genius. I have never fancied myself to be a man of genius, but had I been so I think I might well have subjected myself to these trammels" (*Autobiography*, p. 101).

When Trollope argued in this manner against a deep-seated cultural prejudice, readers and critics tended to take his words at face value. Instead of giving him credit for the courage of his challenge to convention, instead of understanding the combination of self-deprecation and tongue-in-cheek humor that prompted Trollope to exaggerate his position at times, many readers and critics, as we have seen, simply concluded that Trollope was not a genius, that he was not brilliant, inspired, or sensitive enough to create art and therefore had to fall back upon mere craft.

James's complaint that Trollope did not take himself seriously as an artist may be viewed in relation to Trollope's style. His style received at best a kind of back-handed praise from James: "Trollope is not what is called a colourist; still less is he a poet: he is seated on the back of heavy-footed prose. But his accounts of those sentiments which the poets are supposed to have made their own is apt to be as touching as demonstrations more lyrical. . . . [In *The Vicar of Bull-hampton*, Henry Gilmore's] history, which has no more pretensions to style than if it were cut out of yesterday's newspaper, lodges itself in the imagination in all sorts of classic company" (p. 532). For twentieth-century readers with writers like James Joyce before them, it has been easy to assume that the simplicity and transparency of Trollope's style represent a failure to be artistic, but there was self-conscious artistry involved in Trollope's concern for language. As he wrote in the *Autobiography*, "language should be so pellucid that the meaning should be rendered without an effort of the reader;—and not only some propositions of meaning, but the very sense, no more and no less, which the writer has intended to put into his words. . . . The language used should be as ready and as efficient a conductor of the mind of the writer to the mind of the reader as is the electric spark which passes from one battery to another battery" (p. 196). Trollope's artistic concern for language was based not on visual or imagistic qualities, not on the "colourist" approach that James mentions, but on its musical properties. He wrote, "[The novelist's] language must come from him as music comes from the rapid touch of the great performer's fingers; as words come from the mouth of the indignant orator; as letters fly from the fingers of the trained compositor; as the syllables tinkled out by little bells form themselves to the ear of the telegraphist. A man who thinks much of his words as he writes them

will generally leave behind him work that smells of oil" (pp. 148–
49). Each morning he began by "weighing with [his] ear the sound
of the words and phrases" he had written the day before (p. 228).
This intense awareness of the sound of language may not correspond
to James's or other twentieth-century writers' sense of style (Trollope
might have thought their work "smelled of oil"), but certainly Trollope was concerned with the beauty of plain language.

James's charge that Trollope lacked seriousness or self-consciousness
as an artist went beyond the issue of language, however, to include
Trollope's narrators and his occasional reminders of the artifice of his
plots. In these cases, James was correct in sensing the difference between his own and Trollope's views of novel writing and the novelist's
role. James might have made the same complaint about most mid-
Victorian novelists. It can be argued, instead, that James was mistaken—that Trollope's narrator contributes to the reader's sense of realism.[11]

But in any case Trollope exacerbated the criticisms against his own
writing by his obvious delight in making money from his writing and
by his comparisons of a writer to a shoemaker:

There are those who would be ashamed to subject themselves to such a task-
master [his diary and self-imposed discipline for writing], and who think
that the man who works with his imagination should allow himself to wait
till—inspiration moves him. When I have heard such doctrine preached, I
have hardly been able to repress my scorn. To me it would not be more ab-
surd if the shoemaker were to wait for inspiration, or the tallow-chandler for
the divine moment of melting. If the man whose business it is to write has
eaten too many good things, or has drunk too much . . . then his condition
may be unfavourable for work; but so will be the condition of the shoemaker
who has been similarly imprudent. . . . I was once told that the surest aid
to the writing of a book was a piece of cobbler's wax on my chair. I certainly
believe in the cobbler's wax much more than the inspiration. (pp. 102–3)

I had long since convinced myself that in such work as mine the great
secret consisted in acknowledging myself to be bound to rules of labour similar to those which an artisan or a mechanic is forced to obey. A shoemaker
when he has finished one pair of shoes does not sit down and contemplate
his work in idle satisfaction. "There is my pair of shoes finished at last! What
a pair of shoes it is!" The shoemaker who so indulged himself would be without wages half his time. It is the same with a professional writer of books.
(p. 268)

Of all Trollope's bold denials or contraventions of received ideas about literature, this analogy was probably the most inflammatory and ultimately the most damaging. Those it offended were less likely to see how much more complex Trollope's practice was than his theory or how often he made his theoretical statements provocative in order to challenge received opinion. The shoemaker analogy may even have been a form of self-deprecation born out of the insecurity of his youth. In any case, it has hurt Trollope's reputation among those who have been unable to look beyond the surface of the analogy or the deceptively ordinary surfaces of his novels.

James's view was more or less representative of the misgivings about Trollope present in the minds of artists and intellectuals from the time of Trollope's death until halfway through the twentieth century. There were still many people who read Trollope and new editions continued to be printed, but on the whole Trollope's novels continued to be relegated to the second (or lower) rank of literature because of their realism, their supposed lack of art, and their conventionality.[12]

The Modern Reassessment

For convenience, we may date the modern reassessment of Trollope from the late 1960s and early 1970s. The social ferment of the 1960s appears to have alerted some critics to the possibility of more radical or unconventional elements in Trollope than had been seen previously. Robert Polhemus in *The Changing World of Anthony Trollope* (1968) discussed some of the ways in which Trollope challenged accepted notions both in his portrayal of social phenomena and in the complex psychology of his characters. In a similar vein, Ruth apRoberts in *The Moral Trollope* (1971) offered a corrective to the view that Trollope was an unintellectual and conventional writer. She demonstrated the seriousness and intellectual consequence of his ethical philosophy; and though her view of Trollope's situation ethics has been modified by a number of recent critics, apRoberts's work remains tremendously important in showing that the complexity of Trollope's ethical vision went hand in hand with distinctive features of his novels like realism, analogous characters, and analogous plots.

By the late 1970s, the scholarly work on Trollope had increased tremendously; in 1977 and 1978 alone, at least six book-length studies of Trollope's novels were published. While that output has not been equaled in any two-year period since then, there have been at least ten books either with major sections on Trollope or exclusively devoted to Trollope since 1980.[13] One of the most important books of the last decade may be seen also as representative of the contemporary critical view; James Kincaid in *The Novels of Anthony Trollope* (1977) discusses Trollope as both a traditional and a modern novelist, using both the closed plot forms of the older novel and the more open forms we have come to appreciate in the twentieth century. In this view, Trollope is neither a thoroughgoing traditionalist nor an out-and-out modernist in either his aesthetic devices (such as his narrators) or his ethical implications.

This view has been shared or elaborated upon by a number of writers.[14] We now have reason to believe that Trollope's seemingly conventional view of women, for instance, or outsiders, was qualified, perhaps unconsciously, by a deeper sympathy for them, and so he built into his narrator's voice or into his counterbalanced plots enough alternatives to question or modify the traditional view he seemed to hold. We also have reason to believe that his multiple plots with their overt verisimilitude do not simply hold up a mirror to reality; instead they and the narrator's presence subtly manipulate the reader's expectations and conclusions.

Literary theory of the last decade or so has been dominated by post-structuralist theories that often describe realism as naive in its epistemological assumptions—naive in assuming that a writer can "copy" without being selective in interpreting what reality is. So it may seem paradoxical that in the same period there has been a resurgence of interest in Trollope. But perhaps the resurgence has resulted from a broadening and deepening of our understanding of how reading and writing function.[15] We have learned to move beyond simplistic notions—such as that a narrator's intrusion destroys the illusion of reality. We have become less apt to take a writer's words at their face value and so have become better able to see either that Trollope deliberately misrepresented himself or that he misunderstood what he was doing. Because of our increased interest in paradoxes, we have become better able to see how a writer like Trollope may be doing something more complicated than it once seemed or how some of his narrative techniques may have implications opposite to what one would think. Our increased fondness for such complexities, then, has perhaps had an effect in rescuing Trollope from the simplistic kinds of criticism often directed at him by his contemporaries or by the generations that followed them.

Some of this increase in interest may simply reflect growth in the profession of academic criticism, but televised versions of the Palliser and Barchester series, together with an increase in the number of Trollope novels in print, testify to a genuine increase in readers' appreciation for Trollope. The theoretical prejudices we have seen in Trollope's contemporaries or Henry James have been repeated by many critics and readers in the century since Trollope's death and are not likely to disappear altogether. But increasingly, the richness of the characters Trollope depicts and the timelessness of their dilemmas are causing reevaluations of his work. Eventually, Trollope may be accorded a place in the first rank of English novelists.

Notes and References

Chapter One

1. Anthony Trollope, *An Autobiography* (1883; reprint ed. Berkeley: University of California Press, 1978), 1. References to the *Autobiography* are hereafter identified by page number in the text.
2. C. P. Snow, *Trollope* (London: Macmillan & Co., 1975), 9–10, and 22.
3. In the *Autobiography,* 9, Trollope says he thinks he would have "gained the prize," and C. P. Snow concurs in *Trollope,* 28–29.
4. *Sir William Gregory, K.C.M.G. An Autobiography,* ed. Lady Gregory (London: John Murray, 1894), quoted in Michael Sadleir, *Anthony Trollope: A Commentary* (Boston: Houghton Mifflin Co., 1927), 56–57.
5. For further information on Trollope's career in the Post Office, see R. H. Super, *Trollope in the Post Office* (Ann Arbor: University of Michigan Press, 1981).
6. See the *Autobiography,* 35–36.
7. Sadleir, *Commentary,* 129–30.
8. Snow, *Trollope,* 62–63.
9. See John Sutherland, *Victorian Novelists and Publishers* (Chicago: University of Chicago Press, 1976), 140, for an account of this particular transaction and Sutherland's chapter 6 in general on Trollope's negotiations with publishers. Sadleir's *Commentary* also discusses such transactions.
10. See Sadleir's *Commentary,* 288–302, on this and on Trollope's related misfortunes of the late 1860s.
11. Sadleir, *Commentary,* 303–5.
12. For further information on Frederick and his letters to his parents, see P. D. Edwards, *Anthony Trollope's Son in Australia: The Life and Letters of F. J. A. Trollope (1847–1910)* (St. Lucia, Australia: University of Queensland Press, 1982).
13. Julian Hawthorne, *Confessions and Criticisms* (Boston: Ticknor, 1887), 140–143, quoted in N. John Hall, "Trollope the Person," in *Trollope: Centenary Essays,* ed. John Halperin (New York: St. Martin's Press, 1982), 176–77.
14. Hall, "Trollope the Person," 177.

Chapter Two

1. On the themes of social change in the Barchester novels, see Robert M. Polhemus, *The Changing World of Anthony Trollope* (Berkeley: University

121

of California Press, 1968); Hugh L. Hennedy, *Unity in Barsetshire* (The Hague: Mouton, 1971); and U. C. Knoepflmacher, "*Barchester Towers:* The Comedy of Change" in *Laughter and Despair: Readings in Ten Novels of the Victorian Era* (Berkeley: University of California Press, 1971), 25–49.

2. Since there is no standard edition of Trollope's novels to refer to, references to his novels will consist of chapter numbers, hereafter enclosed in parentheses in the text.

3. On the thematic unity of this rather difficult novel, see Hennedy, *Unity,* 71–89.

4. On the difficulties of defining realism, the changing nature of nineteenth-century literary realism, and the self-contradictions within realistic fiction, see George Levine, *The Realistic Imagination: English Fiction from Frankenstein to Lady Chatterley* (Chicago: University of Chicago Press, 1981). On the complexities of Trollope's realism, see David Skilton, *Anthony Trollope and His Contemporaries: A Study in the Theory and Conventions of Mid-Victorian Fiction* (New York: St. Martin's Press, 1972), 137–52; or Walter M. Kendrick, *The Novel-Machine: The Theory and Fiction of Anthony Trollope* (Baltimore: Johns Hopkins University Press, 1980).

5. Nathaniel Hawthorne, letter to Joseph M. Field on 11 February 1860, quoted by Trollope in the *Autobiography,* 122–23.

6. For a discussion of the widening social range of the early Victorian novel, see Kathleen Tillotson, *Novels of the Eighteen-Forties* (London: Oxford University Press, 1961), 73–88.

7. Bishop Connop Thirlwall, "On the Irony of Sophocles," *Philological Museum* 2 (1833): 483–537, quoted in Ruth apRoberts, *The Moral Trollope* (Athens: Ohio University Press, 1971), 38.

8. On the characters' introspection, see Skilton, *Anthony Trollope,* 138–42.

9. Most critics seem to consider Harding a hero, but Coral Lansbury dissents, seeing Harding's resignation as the easy way out of the problem; see *The Reasonable Man: Trollope's Legal Fiction* (Princeton: Princeton University Press, 1981), 128–43.

10. Henry James, "Anthony Trollope," *Century Magazine,* July 1883, reprinted in *Anthony Trollope: The Critical Heritage,* ed. Donald Smalley (New York: Barnes & Noble; London: Routledge & Kegan Paul, 1969), 525–45.

11. As James Kincaid has written, critical opinion about Trollope's narrators has been divided into two camps—those who think the narrators immerse us in the fiction and those who think the narrators distance us from it—but the narrators may be seen to do both; see *The Novels of Anthony Trollope* (Oxford: Clarendon Press, 1977), 32–44. For further discussion of the narrators, see also Richard Fogle, "Illusion, Point of View, and Criticism," in *The Theory of the Novel: New Essays,* ed. John Halperin (New York: Oxford University Press, 1974), 338–52; and Juliet McMaster, *Trollope's Palliser Novels: Theme and Pattern* (New York: Oxford University Press, 1978), chap. 10.

12. Geoffrey Harvey, *The Art of Anthony Trollope* (New York: St. Martin's Press, 1980), 8–9.

13. Kincaid discusses Trollope's use of both open and closed form; see *Novels,* chaps. 1 and 2. The term "open" form comes from J. Hillis Miller, *The Form of Victorian Fiction: Thackeray, Dickens, Trollope, George Eliot, Meredith, and Hardy* (Notre Dame, Ind.: University of Notre Dame Press, 1968).

14. For an important general account of Trollope's use of variation and parallelism, see Jerome Thale, "The Problem of Structure in Trollope," *Nineteenth-Century Fiction* 15 (1960–61):147–57.

15. See Joseph Wiesenfarth, "Dialectics in *Barchester Towers,*" in *Anthony Trollope,* ed. Tony Bareham (New York: Barnes & Noble, 1980), 36–53. On the moral drama of self-deception and discovery, see W. David Shaw, "Moral Drama in *Barchester Towers,*" *Nineteenth-Century Fiction* 19 (1964–65): 45–54.

Chapter Three

1. Critical assessment of Lily and her "perversity" has varied. Although Trollope described her as a "prig" (*Autobiography,* 150), some readers have felt either that he intended her to be altogether admirable or that he was not entirely in control in portraying her; see, for instance, Polhemus, *Changing World,* 94. For somewhat differing discussions of Lily's "perversity," see Kincaid, *Novels,* 125–32; or McMaster, *Palliser Novels,* chap. 1.

2. On the parallel plots and characters, see Hennedy, *Unity,* chap. 5; Kincaid, *Novels,* 125–32; or McMaster, *Palliser Novels,* chap. 1.

3. For discussions of the thematic dimensions of the three parallel plots and their analogous characters, see David S. Chamberlain, "Unity and Irony in Trollope's *Can You Forgive Her?,*" *Studies in English Literature* 8 (1968): 669–80; Kincaid, *Novels,* 181–91; or McMaster, *Palliser Novels,* 20–37.

4. On the ways in which Trollope's sympathy for women's problems permeates his novels, despite his conscious disapproval of the women's rights movement, see Polhemus; Kincaid; and Richard Barickman, Susan MacDonald, and Myra Stark, *Corrupt Relations: Dickens, Thackeray, Trollope, Collins and the Victorian Sexual System* (New York: Columbia University Press, 1982), chaps. 1, 2, and 6. For an argument that Trollope's women do reflect stereotypical notions, see David Aitken, "Anthony Trollope on 'the Genus Girl,' " *Nineteenth-Century Fiction* 28 (1974):417–34.

5. Juliet McMaster discusses the misconceptions that have led a number of critics to dislike the Alice Vavasor plot, dislike Alice herself, or misinterpret Alice's feelings for her two suitors; see *Palliser Novels,* 20–37.

6. For discussions of how Trollope's narrator functions to broaden our perspectives on women even when he appears most conservative, see Kincaid, *Novels,* chaps. 1 and 2; and Barickman, MacDonald, and Stark, *Corrupt Rela-*

tions, chaps. 2 and 6. At the opposite extreme, see John Halperin, *Trollope and Politics: A Study of the Pallisers and Others* (New York: Barnes & Noble, 1977), 34–45, for an interpretation that uses Trollope's external statements on women's rights and his caricatures of feminists to argue that Trollope disapproves of women like Alice.

7. On the theme of public versus private, see Chamberlain, "Unity and Irony," and Kincaid, *Novels,* 181–91.

8. Polhemus, *Changing World,* 104.

9. Polhemus, *Changing World,* 112.

Chapter Four

1. This ambivalence leads to varying critical interpretations—e.g., Robert Polhemus views the focus on retribution as a regrettable lapse into conventional morality by a writer who ordinarily stresses moral complexity. See *Changing World,* 87.

2. John Ruskin, "Of Queen's Gardens," in *The Works of John Ruskin,* ed. E. T. Cook and Alexander Wedderburn, vol. 18 (London: George Allen, 1905). See also Walter E. Houghton, *The Victorian Frame of Mind: 1830–1870* (New Haven, Conn.: Yale University Press, 1957), chap. 13.

3. On the theme of commercialism, see Robert Martin Adams, *"Orley Farm* and Real Fiction," *Nineteenth-Century Fiction* 8 (1953–54):27–41.

4. The Phineas novels may be considered together since Trollope said they were, in fact, one novel (*Autobiography,* 265), but they were not written at the same time; *Phineas Finn* was written in 1866–67 and *Phineas Redux* in 1870–71.

5. For further discussions of Laura, see Ramona L. Denton, " 'That Cage' of Femininity: Trollope's Lady Laura," *South Atlantic Bulletin* 45 (1980):1–10; Juliet McMaster, *Palliser Novels;* or Barickman, MacDonald, and Stark, *Corrupt Relations.* On the subject of love in the Phineas novels, see Robert M. Polhemus, "Being in Love in *Phineas Finn/Phineas Redux:* Desire, Devotion, Consolation," *Nineteenth-Century Fiction* 37 (1982–83):383–95.

6. Lizzie's fondness for Byron should be seen in the context of Trollope's attitude toward Byron; see Donald Stone, "Trollope, Byron, and the Conventionalities," in *The Worlds of Victorian Fiction,* ed. Jerome Buckley (Cambridge, Mass.: Harvard University Press, 1975), 179–203.

7. For a more extensive discussion of this theme and of the minor characters, see McMaster, *Palliser Novels,* chap. 5.

Chapter Five

1. On the interrelation of the London and other subplots to the Crawley plot, see Thale, "The Problem of Structure" and Harvey, *Art of Trollope,* 54–73.

2. See, for example, Polhemus, *Changing World,* 129–38.
3. See, for example, Kincaid, *Novels,* 132–42.
4. On situation ethics see apRoberts, *The Moral Trollope.*
5. Kincaid, *Novels,* 10–18.
6. On the dynamics of power in relation to sex roles in this novel, see Christopher Herbert, "*He Knew He Was Right,* Mrs. Lynn Linton, and the Duplicities of Victorian Marriage," *Texas Studies in Language and Literature* 25 (1983):448–69. See also Ruth apRoberts, "Emily and Nora and Dorothy and Priscilla and Jemima and Carry," in *The Victorian Experience: The Novelists,* ed. Richard A. Levine (Athens: Ohio University Press, 1976), 87–120; and Simon Gatrell, "Jealousy, Mastery, Love and Madness: A Brief Reading of *He Knew He Was Right,*" in *Trollope,* ed. Bareham, 95–115. On Trevelyan's isolation, see Stone, "Trollope, Byron."

Chapter Six

1. For a discussion of changing social mobility and deference in Trollope's novels, see Asa Briggs, *Victorian People: A Reassessment of Persons and Themes 1851–67,* rev. ed. (Chicago: University of Chicago Press, 1970), chap. 4.
2. See Sadleir, *Trollope,* 288–302, on Trollope's disappointments during this period; see Halperin, *Trollope and Politics,* chap. 5, on the Beverley election. A. O. J. Cockshut in *Anthony Trollope: A Critical Study* (1955; reprint ed. New York: New York University Press, 1968) discussed the late novels under the heading "Progress to Pessimism," and critics have debated Cockshut's description ever since.
3. The most helpful guide to the relation between actual political issues and Trollope's fictionalized ones is Halperin, *Trollope and Politics.* See his chap. 7 on *Phineas Redux.*
4. Halperin, ibid., 159–60, explains how Trollope's portrait of Emilius may be explained by his dislike of Disraeli.
5. For further discussion on the fascinating Madame Max, see McMaster, *Palliser Novels;* in light of the vague suggestions of her Jewish background, see Anne Aresty Naman, *The Jew in the Victorian Novel: Some Relationships between Prejudice and Art* (New York: AMS Press, 1980), 106–17.
6. For further discussion of how Trollope develops his themes through analogies and parallels in this novel, see Robert Tracy, *Trollope's Later Novels,* (Berkeley: University of California Press, 1978), chap. 5.
7. Tony Tanner discusses the relevance of the emergence of modern capitalism in "Trollope's *The Way We Live Now:* Its Modern Significance," *Critical Quarterly* 9 (1967):256–71. Robin Gilmour is helpful on how outsiders like Melmotte and Mrs. Hurtle are treated with a combination of distrust and understanding; see "A Lesser Thackeray? Trollope and the Victorian Novel," in *Trollope,* ed. Bareham, 182–203. See also Bill Overton, *The Unof-*

ficial Trollope (Sussex, England: Harvester Press, 1982) on the difference between Trolloope's official and unofficial views. For a discussion of the Jew as outsider in relation to Melmotte, see Edgar Rosenberg, *From Shylock To Svengali: Jewish Stereotypes in English Fiction* (Stanford: Stanford University Press, 1960), 140–50; or Naman, *The Jew,* 128–48.

8. As the story progresses, however, Marie grows better able to judge others; see R. D. McMaster, "Women in *The Way We Live Now,*" *English Studies in Canada* 7 (1981):68–80, for an interesting discussion of both Marie and Georgiana. See also Rosenberg, *Shylock,* 147–50.

9. Gilmour, "Lesser Thackeray."

10. For further insight into the political dimension of *The Prime Minister,* see Halperin, *Trollope and Politics,* 211–45. See McMaster, *Palliser Novels,* 103–28 and Kincaid, *Novels,* 216–25, for further discussion of the parallel plots.

12. See Halperin, *Trollope and Politics,* 236, on how Trollope's dislike for Disraeli is involved in his negative portrait of Lopez. See also Naman, *The Jew,* 148–60.

12. See, for instance, Polhemus on the Whartonses' cruelty to Lopez, *Changing World,* 197–209. My argument here may be seen as an extension of the argument that Robin Gilmour has made about Trollope's conservatism and sympathy for outsiders in *The Way We Live Now;* see "Lesser Thackeray."

Chapter Seven

1. On situation ethics in Trollope, see apRoberts, *Moral Trollope;* for an opposing argument, see Roger Slakey, "Trollope's Case for the Moral Imperative," *Nineteenth-Century Fiction* 28 (1973):305–20.

2. Virginia Woolf, *The Common Reader,* First Series (London: Hogarth Press, 1925), 213.

3. Cockshut writes, "The story of Mary Lovelace is, in the main, an analysis of the suffering inflicted on women by mild and well-meaning men," *Trollope,* 154. For further discussion of the problems of marriage in *Is He Popenjoy?,* see Barickman, MacDonald, and Stark, *Corrupt Relations,* 196–98; or apRoberts, *Moral Trollope,* 161–65.

4. Unsigned Notice, *Saturday Review,* 1 June 1878, in *Critical Heritage,* ed. Smalley, 440.

5. John Hagan, *"The Duke's Children:* Trollope's Psychological Masterpiece," *Nineteenth-Century Fiction* 13 (1958):5.

6. Ibid., 2.

7. It seems appropriate here to refer to the parent as "he" since most of the drama of parenthood in the late Trollope concerns fathers; the case of Mrs. Bolton is exceptional and follows a different pattern from the cases of fatherly disappointment.

8. Kincaid, *Novels,* 231–32.

9. Hagan, "Psychological Masterpiece," 1–21; on this theme, see also McMaster, *Palliser Novels,* chap. 7.

10. Cockshut develops the theme of pessimism in the late novels by describing *Ayala's Angel* as an anomaly, a novel similar to Trollope's novels of the early sixties (*Trollope,* 198). For descriptions of *Ayala's Angel* as romance or comedy, see Kincaid, *Novels,* 256–60; Andrew Wright, *Anthony Trollope: Dream and Art* (London: Macmillan & Co., 1983), 141–47; and Tracy, *Later Novels,* 244–51.

11. See Kendrick, *Novel Machine,* 103–5; and J. Hillis Miller, *Form of Victorian Fiction,* 124–139. Tracy, *Later Novels,* 244–51, finds undercutting of a different kind than Kendrick and Miller.

12. Northrop Frye, *Anatomy of Criticism* (Princeton: Princeton University Press, 1957), 163. The fullest discussion of Trollope's use of comedy is Kincaid's *Novels.*

13. See Kendrick, *Novel Machine,* 103–5, and Miller, *Form of Victorian Fiction,* 124–39.

14. For judicious comments on the critical disagreements about Mr. Scarborough, see Roger Slakey, "Moral Imperative," 305–20; and Robert Tracy, *Later Novels,* 295–311. For an interesting recent treatment of the novel, see Geoffrey Harvey, "A Parable of Justice: Drama and Rhetoric in *Mr. Scarborough's Family,*" *Nineteenth-Century Fiction* 37 (1982–83):419–29.

15. Slakey, "Moral Imperative," 316–17.

Chapter Eight

1. Bradford Booth, *Anthony Trollope: Aspects of His Life and Art* (Bloomington: Indiana University Press, 1958), 229.

2. Richard Holt Hutton, *Spectator* 9 December 1882, in *Critical Heritage,* ed. Smalley, 505–6. For further information on Trollope's contemporaries' reactions to his novels, see Skilton, *Trollope and His Contemporaries.*

3. Nathaniel Hawthorne, in Trollope's *Autobiography,* 122.

4. Unsigned review, *Examiner,* 20 April 1861, in *Critical Heritage,* ed. Smalley, 118.

5. Unsigned notice, *Saturday Review,* 4 May 1861, in *Critical Heritage,* ed. Smalley, 122 and 124–5.

6. Hutton, in *Critical Heritage,* ed. Smalley, 506.

7. Unsigned essay, *Times,* 7 December 1882, in *Critical Heritage,* ed. Smalley, 502.

8. For a fuller discussion of how Trollope's reputation has suffered from aesthetic assumptions appropriate for writers like James, Joyce, and others, see apRoberts, *Moral Trollope,* chap. one.

9. Henry James, "Anthony Trollope," 525. Further references to the Smalley reprint of this essay (see chap. 2, n. 10) will appear in parentheses in my text.

10. For evidence that Trollope's account of his own composing habits misrepresented the amount of his creative effort, see John A. Sutherland, "Trollope at Work on *The Way We Live Now*," *Nineteenth-Century Fiction* 37 (1982–83):472–93. See also Booth, *Trollope*, chap. 1; or Hall, "Trollope the Person," on Trollope's willingness to misrepresent himself in social situations.

11. See, for instance, Fogle, "Illusion, Point of View, and Criticism," 338–52. McMaster, *Palliser Novels;* Kincaid, *Novels;* and Harvey, *Art of Trollope,* are also helpful on this issue.

12. See N. John Hall, Introduction to *The Trollope Critics* (Totowa, N.J.: Barnes & Noble, 1981), vii–xiii, on the editions of Trollope's novels in the thirty years after his death and what those editions demonstrate about his readership.

13. Donald Stone reports that there were as many books on Trollope published between 1976 and 1981 as had been published in the ninety-six years after his death; see "Trollope Studies, 1976–1981," *Dickens Studies Annual* 11 (1983):313.

14. See, for instance, Harvey, *Art of Trollope;* Gilmour, "Lesser Thackeray"; Barickman, MacDonald, and Stark, *Corrupt Relations;* and Overton, *Unofficial Trollope.*

15. For a poststructuralist discussion of the implications and contradictions within Trollope's theory of novel writing, see Kendrick, *The Novel Machine.* See also Levine, *The Realistic Imagination,* for a poststructuralist discussion of the complexities of realism (marred, however, by Levine's finding Trollope one of the least interesting of nineteenth-century realists).

Selected Bibliography

PRIMARY SOURCES

1. Novels
   The entry cites the first book publication in England followed by the dates of the original serial run in parentheses. The source for most of this information is Michael Sadleir's *Bibliography* (see below). There is no standard edition of Trollope's novels. Many are available in Oxford's World Classics editions. Penguin also publishes many titles, and Dover Press and Arno Press have recently published a number of the once hard-to-find novels.

The Macdermots of Ballycloran. 3 vols. London: T. C. Newby, 1847.

The Kellys and the O'Kellys. 3 vols. London: Henry Colburn, 1848.

La Vendée: An Historical Romance. 3 vols. London: Henry Colburn, 1850.

The Warden. London: Longman, 1855.

Barchester Towers. 3 vols. London: Longman, 1857.

The Three Clerks: A Novel. 3 vols. London: Bentley, 1858.

Doctor Thorne: A Novel. 3 vols. London: Chapman & Hall, 1858.

The Bertrams: A Novel. 3 vols. London: Chapman & Hall, 1859.

Castle Richmond: A Novel. 3 vols. London: Chapman & Hall, 1860.

Framley Parsonage. 3 vols. London: Smith, Elder & Co., 1861. (*Cornhill,* January 1860–April 1861).

Orley Farm. 2 vols. London: Chapman & Hall, 1862. (20 nos., March 1861–October 1862, Chapman & Hall).

The Struggles of Brown, Jones and Robinson: by One of the Firm. 1 vol. New York: Harper & Brothers, 1862. First English ed. London: Smith, Elder & Co., 1870. (*Cornhill,* August 1861–March 1862).

Rachel Ray: A Novel. 2 vols. London: Chapman & Hall, 1863.

The Small House at Allington. 2 vols. London: Smith, Elder & Co., 1864. (*Cornhill,* September 1862–April 1864).

Can You Forgive Her? 2 vols. London: Chapman & Hall, 1864. (20 nos., January 1864–August 1865, Chapman & Hall).

Miss Mackenzie. 2 vols. London: Chapman & Hall, 1865.

The Belton Estate. 3 vols. London: Chapman & Hall, 1866. (*Fortnightly Review,* May 1865–January 1866).

Nina Balatka. 2 vols. Edinburgh: Blackwood, 1867. (*Blackwood's,* July 1866–January 1867).

The Last Chronicle of Barset. 2 vols. London: Smith, Elder & Co., 1867. (32 nos., December 1866–July 1867, Smith, Elder & Co.).

The Claverings. 2 vols. London: Smith, Elder & Co., 1867. (*Cornhill,* February 1866–May 1867).

Linda Tressel. 2 vols. Edinburgh: Blackwood, 1868. (*Blackwood's,* October 1867–May 1868).

Phineas Finn, The Irish Member. 2 vols. London: Virtue, 1869. (*Saint Paul's,* October 1867–May 1869).

He Knew He Was Right. 2 vols. London: Strahan, 1869. (32 nos., October 1868–May 1869, Virtue).

The Vicar of Bullhampton. London: Bradbury, Evans, 1870. (July 1869–May 1870, Bradbury, Evans).

Sir Harry Hotspur of Humblethwaite. London: Hurst & Blackett, 1871.

Ralph the Heir. 3 vols. London: Hurst & Blackett, 1871. (19 nos., January 1870–July 1871, Strahan, and as supplement to *Saint Paul's Magazine*).

The Golden Lion of Granpère. London: Tinsley, 1872. (*Good Words,* January 1872–August 1872).

The Eustace Diamonds. 3 vols. London: Chapman & Hall, 1873. (*Fortnightly Review,* July 1871–February 1873).

Phineas Redux. 2 vols. London: Chapman & Hall, 1874. (*Graphic,* July 1873–January 1874).

Lady Anna. 2 vols. London: Chapman & Hall, 1874. (*Fortnightly Review,* April 1873–April 1874).

Harry Heathcote of Gangoil: A Tale of Australian Bush Life. London: Sampson Low, 1874. (*Graphic,* December 1873).

The Way We Live Now. 2 vols. London: Chapman & Hall, 1875. (20 nos., February 1874–September 1875, Chapman & Hall).

The Prime Minister. 2 vols. London: Chapman & Hall, 1876. (8 nos., November 1875–June 1876, Chapman & Hall).

The American Senator. 3 vols. London: Chapman & Hall, 1877. (*Temple Bar,* May 1876–July 1877).

Is He Popenjoy?: A Novel. 3 vols. London: Chapman & Hall, 1878. (*All the Year Round,* October 1877–July 1878).

An Eye for an Eye. 2 vols. London: Chapman & Hall, 1879. (*Whitehall Review,* August 1878–February 1879).

John Caldigate. 3 vols. London: Chapman & Hall, 1879. (*Blackwood's,* April 1878–June 1879).

Cousin Henry: A Novel. 2 vols. London: Chapman & Hall, 1879. (*Manchester Weekly Times* and the *North British Weekly Mail,* March 1879–May 1879).

The Duke's Children: A Novel. 2 vols. London: Chapman & Hall, 1880. (*All the Year Round,* October 1879–July 1880).

Doctor Wortle's School: A Novel. 2 vols. London: Chapman & Hall, 1881. (*Blackwood's,* May 1880–December 1880).

Ayala's Angel. 3 vols. London: Chapman & Hall, 1881.

Marion Fay: A Novel. 3 vols. London: Chapman & Hall, 1882. (*Graphic*, December 1881–June 1882).

Kept in the Dark: A Novel. 2 vols. London: Chatto & Windus, 1882. (*Good Words*, May 1882–December 1882).

The Fixed Period: A Novel. 2 vols. Edinburgh: Blackwood, 1882. (*Blackwood's*, October 1881–March 1882).

Mr. Scarborough's Family. 3 vols. London: Chatto & Windus, 1883. (*All the Year Round*, May 1882–June 1883).

The Landleaguers. 3 vols. London: Chatto & Windus, 1883. (*Life*, November 1882–October 1883).

An Old Man's Love. 2 vols. Edinburgh: Blackwood, 1883.

2. Travel Books

The West Indies and the Spanish Main. London: Chapman & Hall, 1859.

North America. 2 vols. London: Chapman & Hall, 1862.

Travelling Sketches. London: Chapman & Hall, 1866. (*Pall Mall Gazette*, August–September 1865).

Australia and New Zealand. 2 vols. London: Chapman & Hall, 1873.

South Africa. 2 vols. London: Chapman & Hall, 1878.

How the "Mastiffs" Went to Iceland. London: Virtue, 1878.

3. Essays and Lectures

Hunting Sketches. London: Chapman & Hall, 1865. (*Pall Mall Gazette*, February 1865–March 1865).

Clergyman of the Church of England. London: Chapman & Hall, 1866. (*Pall Mall Gazette*, November 1865–January 1866).

The Commentaries of Caesar. Edinburgh: Blackwood, 1870.

Thackeray. London: Macmillan & Co., 1879.

The Life of Cicero. 2 vols. London: Chapman & Hall, 1880.

Lord Palmerston, English Political Leaders. London: Isbister, 1882.

An Autobiography. 2 vols. Edinburgh: Blackwood, 1883. Reprints. Berkeley: University of California Press, 1947, 1978.

The New Zealander. Edited by N. John Hall. Oxford: Oxford University Press, 1972.

Four Lectures. Edited by Morris L. Parrish. London: Constable, 1938.

Miscellaneous Essays and Reviews. Edited by Michael Y. Mason. New York: Arno Press, 1981.

Writings for Saint Paul's Magazine. Edited by John Sutherland. New York: Arno Press, 1981.

4. Collections of Stories

Trollope's stores are now most accessible either through the Arno Press or the Texas Christian Press series of reprints.

Tales of All Countries [First Series]. London: Chapman & Hall, 1861.
Tales of All Countries: Second Series. London: Chapman & Hall, 1863. (*Public Opinion, London Review,* and *Illustrated London News,* January–December 1861).
Lotta Schmidt: and Other Stories. London: Strahan, 1867.
An Editor's Tales. London: Strahan, 1870. (*St. Paul's,* October 1869–May 1870).
Why Frau Frohmann Raised Her Prices: And Other Stories. London: Isbister, 1882.
The Two Heroines of Plumplington. New York: Oxford University Press, 1954. (*Good Words,* 25 December 1882).

5. Correspondence
The Letters of Anthony Trollope. 2 vols. Edited by N. John Hall. Stanford: Stanford University Press, 1983.

SECONDARY SOURCES

1. Bibliographies

Ford, George H., ed. *Victorian Fiction: A Second Guide to Research.* New York: Modern Language Association, 1978. Ruth apRoberts surveys work done on Trollope after Smalley's review in Stevenson (below).
Lyons, Anne K. *Anthony Trollope: An Annotated Bibliography of Periodical Works by and about Him in the United States and Great Britain to 1900.* Greenwood, Fl: Penkevill Publishing Co., 1985.
Olmstead, John Charles and **Welch, Jeffrey Egan.** *The Reputation of Trollope: An Annotated Bibliography, 1925–1975.* New York: Garland, 1978. Contains 652 annotated items with selections from reviewers.
Sadleir, Michael. *Trollope: A Bibliography: An Analysis of the History and Structure of the Works of Anthony Trollope, and a General Survey of the Effect of Original Publishing Conditions on a Book's Subsequent Rarity.* London: Constable, 1928: Reprint. London: Dawsons, 1964. The definitive bibliography of Trollope's writings.
Stevenson, Lionel, ed. *Victorian Fiction: A Guide to Research.* Cambridge, Mass.: Harvard University Press, 1964. Contains a review essay by Donald Smalley of work on Trollope up to 1962.
Stone, Donald D. "Trollope Studies, 1976–1981." *Dickens Studies Annual* 11 (1983):313–33. Surveys work done on Trollope since apRoberts's review in Ford.

2. Books and Parts of Books
This list concentrates on more recent Trollope criticism.

apRoberts, Ruth. *The Moral Trollope*. Athens: Ohio University Press, 1971; London: Chatto & Windus, 1971. (Published in England as *Trollope: Artist and Moralist*.) A study of Trollope's moral concerns and intellectual background, particularly important for its discussion of situation ethics and aesthetics.

Bareham, Tony, ed. *Anthony Trollope*. New York: Barnes & Noble, 1980. A collection of essays on a range of issues and novels.

Barickman, Richard; MacDonald, Susan; and Stark, Myra. *Corrupt Relations: Dickens, Thackeray, Trollope, Collins and the Victorian Sexual System*. New York: Columbia University Press, 1982. Discusses Trollope's presentation of women and sexual relations in connection with conventions of the Victorian novel.

Booth, Bradford. *Anthony Trollope: Aspects of His Life and Art*. Bloomington: Indiana University Press, 1958. Historically important both as an attempt to reestablish Trollope's importance and for the limitations in Booth's interpretation it reveals.

Briggs, Asa. "Trollope, Bagehot and the English Constitution." In *Victorian People: A Reassessment of Persons and Themes, 1851–67*, 87–115. Rev. ed. Chicago: University of Chicago Press, 1970. A historian's view of Trollope's political views.

Cockshut, A. O. J. *Anthony Trollope: A Critical Study*. London: Collins, 1955: Reprint. New York: New York University Press, 1968. Still valuable, though not wholly reliable, articulation of the late Trollope's pessimism.

Edwards, P. D. *Anthony Trollope, His Art and Scope*. St. Lucia, Australia: University of Queensland Press, 1977. Useful for its clarification of the role of the sensational in Trollope's realism.

Garrett, Peter K. *The Victorian Multiplot Novel: Studies in Dialogical Form*. New Haven: Yale University Press, 1980. Discusses the tensions between unifying and decentralizing structural and narrative principles in the Victorian novel, with close analysis of two Trollope novels.

Gerould, Winifred Gregory and Gerould, James Thayer. *A Guide to Trollope*. Contains helpful record of characters and places in the novels.

Hall, N. John. *The Trollope Critics*. Totowa, N.J.: Barnes & Noble, 1981. Useful collection of older and often hard to find appreciations of Trollope, along with an informative introduction, a good bibliography, and important recent essays.

Halperin, John. *Trollope and Politics: A Study of the Pallisers and Others*. New York: Barnes & Noble, 1977. The most extensive study to date of the political background and its influence on Trollope's novels.

———, ed. *Trollope: Centenary Essays*. New York: St Martin's Press, 1982. A collection of essays on facets of Trollope's work.

Harvey, Geoffrey. *The Art of Anthony Trollope*. New York: St. Martin's

Press, 1980. Helpful on Trollope's debt to Jacobean drama, his critique
of Victorian society, and his narrative devices.

Hennedy, Hugh L. *Unity in Barsetshire.* The Hague: Mouton, 1971. Contains insights into individual novels in the Barsetshire series, even if
some of the overall claims may be questionable.

Kendrick, Walter. *The Novel Machine: The Theory and Fiction of Anthony
Trollope.* Baltimore: John Hopkins University Press, 1980. Important
exploration of Trollope's realism and statements about writing in the
light of poststructuralist theory, though at times difficult reading.

Kincaid, James. *The Novels of Anthony Trollope.* Oxford: Clarendon Press,
1977. Valuable readings of all the novels but particularly important for
its discussion of form and convention.

Knoepflmacher, U. C. *Laughter and Despair: Readings in Ten Novels of the
Victorian Era.* Berkeley: University of California Press, 1971. Illuminating close reading of *Barchester Towers* and description of Trollope's use
of comedy.

Lansbury, Coral. *The Reasonable Man: Trollope's Legal Fiction.* Princeton:
Princeton University Press, 1981. Discusses the influence on Trollope's
fiction of Post Office report writing, legal modes of argument, and the
presentation of evidence.

Levine, George. *The Realistic Imagination: English Fiction from Frankenstein to
Lady Chatterley.* Chicago: University of Chicago Press, 1981. Helpful
study of the tensions in the tradition of realism, though Trollope's realism is presented as technically uninteresting.

McMaster, Juliet. *Trollope's Palliser Novels: Theme and Pattern.* New York:
Oxford University Press, 1978. Detailed and insightful readings of the
Palliser novels.

Miller, J. Hillis, *The Form of Victorian Fiction: Thackeray, Dickens, Trollope,
George Eliot, Meredith, and Hardy.* Notre Dame, Ind.: University of
Notre Dame Press, 1968. Important for its study of the narrator and
the exploration of selfhood in Trollope.

Overton, Bill. *The Unofficial Trollope.* Sussex, England: Harvester Press,
1982. Helpful discussion of the tensions in Trollope's work between
conventional views and more unconventional, "unofficial" views.

Polhemus, Robert M. *The Changing World of Anthony Trollope.* Berkeley:
University of California Press, 1968. Chronological study of the novels,
emphasizing Trollope's depictions of social change. Important in revising the older view of Trollope as upholder of the status quo.

Sadleir, Michael. *Trollope: A Commentary.* Boston: Houghton Mifflin Co.,
1927. Still in most respects the best biography.

Skilton, David. *Anthony Trollope and His Contemporaries: A Study in the Theory
and Conventions of Mid-Victorian Fiction.* New York: St. Martin's Press,
1972. Helpful background information on Trollope's reputation and the
reading tastes of his public.

Smalley, Donald, ed. *Anthony Trollope: The Critical Heritage.* New York: Barnes & Noble; London: Routledge & Kegan Paul, 1969. Contains 253 reviews by Trollope's contemporaries of the novels at the time of their publication.

Snow, C. P. *Trollope.* London: Macmillan & Co., 1975. Brief biography with the useful insights of a fellow novelist.

Super, R. H. *Trollope in the Post Office.* Ann Arbor: University of Michigan Press, 1981. Brings to light new facts about Trollope's career in the Post Office.

Sutherland, John. *Victorian Novelists and Publishers.* Chicago: University of Chicago Press, 1976. Informative about Trollope's dealings with publishers.

Tracy, Robert. *Trollope's Later Novels.* Berkeley: University of California Press, 1978. Studies the structural dimensions of Trollope's multiple plots in the late novels.

Wright, Andrew. *Anthony Trollope: Dream and Art.* London: Macmillan & Co. 1983. Sensible readings of the more important novels.

3. Articles

Aitken, David. "Anthony Trollope on 'the Genus Girl.' " *Nineteenth-Century Fiction* 28 (1974):417–34. Shows that Trollope's sympathetic portraits of women are not free of stereotypes.

apRoberts, Ruth. "Emily and Nora and Dorothy and Priscilla and Jemima and Carry." In *The Victorian Experience: The Novelists,* edited by Richard A. Levine, 87–120. Athens: Ohio University Press, 1976. Discusses sexual relations in *He Knew He Was Right* in light of the status of women in Victorian England.

Chamberlain, David S. "Unity and Irony in Trollope's *Can You Forgive Her?*" *Studies in English Literature* 8 (1968):669–80. Useful for understanding how the three plots balance and reinforce each other.

Denton, Ramona L. " 'That Cage' of Femininity: Trollope's Lady Laura." *South Atlantic Bulletin* 45 (1980):1–10. Trollope's insight and sympathy in portraying Laura's plight is viewed in relation to women's roles.

Fogle, Richard Harter. "Illusion, Point of View, and Criticism." In *The Theory of the Novel: New Essays,* edited by John Halperin, 338–52. New York: Oxford University Press, 1974. Helpful discussion of the flaws in much of the criticism of Trollope's narrator.

Hagan, John. "*The Duke's Children:* Trollope's Psychological Masterpiece." *Nineteenth-Century Fiction* 13 (1958):1–21. Still the most important article on this topic.

Herbert, Christopher. "*He Knew He Was Right,* Mrs. Lynn Linton, and the Duplicities of Victorian Marriage." *Texas Studies in Language and Literature* 25 (1983):448–69. Examines contradictions in the Victorian view of marriage and how Trollope's exploration of marriage is more complex than contemporary melodramatic treatment.

Polhemus, Robert M. "Being in Love in *Phineas Finn/Phineas Redux:* Desire, Devotion, Consolation." *Nineteenth-Century Fiction* 37 (1982–83):383–95. Discusses the larger ramifications of the novels' preoccupation with love.

Slakey, Roger. "Trollope's Case for the Moral Imperative." *Nineteenth-Century Fiction* 28 (1973):305–20. A study of the ethical implications of Trollope's novels. Contains a useful corrective to the idea that Trollope is a relativist.

Stone, Donald D. "Trollope, Byron, and the Conventionalities." In *The Worlds of Victorian Fiction,* edited by Jerome Buckley, 179–203. Cambridge: Harvard University Press, 1975. Shows how Trollope explores in his characters both the lure and danger of the romantic values Byron represented.

Sutherland, John A. "Trollope at Work on *The Way We Live Now.*" *Nineteenth-Century Fiction* 37 (1982–83):472–93. Demonstrates that Trollope's composing practices were more complex and creative than he described them as being.

Thale, Jerome. "The Problem of Structure in Trollope." *Nineteenth-Century Fiction* 15 (1960–61):147–57. Still important discussion of Trollope's use of parallels and repetitions in events and characters.

Index

ALSO BY JON WINOKUR

Mondo Canine
Friendly Advice
A Curmudgeon's Garden of Love
Zen to Go
The Portable Curmudgeon
Writers on Writing

COMPILED AND EDITED BY
Jon Winokur

TRUE CONFESSIONS

A DUTTON BOOK

DUTTON
Published by the Penguin Group
Penguin Books USA Inc.,
375 Hudson Street, New York, New York 10014, U.S.A.
Penguin Books Ltd, 27 Wrights Lane, London W8 5TZ, England
Penguin Books Australia Ltd, Ringwood, Victoria, Australia
Penguin Books Canada Ltd,
10 Alcorn Avenue, Toronto, Ontario, Canada M4V 3B2
Penguin Books (N.Z.) Ltd,
182–190 Wairau Road, Auckland 10, New Zealand

Penguin Books Ltd, Registered Offices:
Harmondsworth, Middlesex, England

First published by Dutton, an imprint of New American Library,
a division of Penguin Books USA Inc.
Distributed in Canada by McClelland & Stewart Inc.

First Printing, July, 1992
10 9 8 7 6 5 4 3 2 1

Acknowledgments for permission to reprint are listed on page 275.

 REGISTERED TRADEMARK—MARCA REGISTRADA

Library of Congress Cataloging in Publication Data
True confessions / compiled and edited by Jon Winoker.
p.   cm.
ISBN 0-525-93466-9
1. Aphorisms and apothegms. I. Winoker, Jon.
PN6269.A2T78   1992
082—dc20   92-3300   CIP

Printed in the United States of America
Set in Melior
Designed by Barbara Huntley

CONTENTS